KEMBALI ~ INTO UNCHARTERED WATERS

JAN TAKI

Published by **Pouldrew Press**,

Portlaw, Co. Waterford, Ireland.

Email: **pouldrewpress@gmail.com**

ISBN: 978-0-9570525-1-2

Printed by Imprint Digital, Exeter in the UK on paper from sustainable forests.

Proofing, typesetting & cover design: **eimear@wordworks.net**

From the Author

This book continues the semi-autobiographical story that I started in 'Kembali ~ The Mystic Returns'. Once again, my tale is enlivened with a huge dollop of fantasy and a large pinch of mischief.

Ride with me on the Grey Winds that take me back to my native Japan to close that chapter of my past life, on to Papua New Guinea, and into the undersea palace of Ratu Kidul, Queen of the Southern Seas, there to do battle and encounter more Mystic forces and Teachings.

Many of the characters in my story were real when they existed in their time and some new ones came a-calling in the middle of my sleepless nights, begging inclusion into my story

Read on!

This book is written for my Choo Kim, Anastasia, Alexander and Christian.

Dedicated to the memory of Tibbs and George Fernandez, Harry Menon, Denis De Silva, and Yoshikazu Kumamoto.

With love and thanks.......

Glossary

***Kembali ~ Into Unchartered Waters* is the second part of a story in two volumes. For those who missed the first book, *Kembali ~ Return Of The Mystic*, here is an explanation of the terms and an introduction to the main characters.**

Ah Jan (later known as Si Jan and Jepun): the main character is a boy reborn to a family in Singapore, just after the Second World War. Ah Jan has a memory of a former life as an Officer in the Imperial Japanese Army. He sets about trying to trace his Past Life, and, in the process, meets a bunch of Mystics who guide him in that direction, while transforming him into a Mystic as well. 'Si' (as in 'Si Jan') is a title given to any man worthy of respect, usually a mature male, while 'Ah' (as in 'Ah Jan') is a term of endearment.

Aweh: one of Si Jan's Mystic Masters, his friend and companion, who can still kill on the human plane. He shows Si Jan how the future can be accessed and even changed.

Badang: another of Si Jan's Mystic Masters, Badang teaches Si Jan the art of remote healing, not only of people, but everything —be it plant, rock, animal or human.

Fat Aunt: Si Jan's cook who becomes his first Master and teaches him the Secrets of the Mau San or Chinese Shamanism, which results in his first near-fatal attempt at Invisibility.

Datok: ancient Chief and Governor of that part of Hari Kong.

Grey Winds: These are the Magic Winds that criss-cross the world, providing Mystics, be they Good or Bad, with a convenient way to travel.

Hari Kong: This is the extra day in a week for Mystics, also known as the 'Eighth Day'. Invisible to the uninitiated, it is a place in between mortal time; Mystics can retreat into Hari Kong to become invisible, to find space to heal themselves, to travel unnoticed or do battle amongst themselves.

Kanemoto: This is the name of the Japanese sword that Kyai Aweng changes into when ordered. It bears the name of its maker, Kanemoto, a famous swordsmith in old Japan.

Kembali: means 'return' in Malay.

Kriyat: name of an invisible spear, given by Pak Samad to Si Jan that only appears when summoned; it always does Si Jan's bidding.

Kyai Aweng: name of the magic keris that Aweh makes for Si

Jan. Forged with his bare hands when the metal was still red hot, it has the power to transform itself into any other weapon Si Jan needs in his battles with the Evil Forces.

Mat Hijau and Rahim: the two 'were tigers' that help Si Jan become invulnerable after capturing the Spirit of Cane.

Nosey, Johnny, Ramasamy, Ah Chee And Mong Hiang: childhood friends of Si Jan.

Pak Samad: the legendary warrior Hang Tuah, he was also the Laksamana or Admiral during the Malaccan Sultanate in the 15th Century. He is now in disguise to lure Si Jan deeper into the Realms of Mysticism.

Princess of Gunong Ledang: Known in Malaysian Legends as the Ruler of the sacred mountain, Mt. Ophir, she is rumoured to have married Hang Tuah.

Spirit of Cane: a magical piece of petrified wood, ritually extracted from a rattan jungle cane and inserted under the skin of the recipient, the 'Spirit of Cane' makes the subject invulnerable to metal.

Sri Pelangi or "Sri": a pretty lady-in-waiting to the Princess who agrees to marry Ah Jan.

See also pages 161 and 162 for background information on the weapons that form part of this story.

Chapter One

My father was waiting at the door when I walked up the driveway. "How was your trip?" he asked after giving me a hug.

"Good, better than I expected," I told him.

"Ah Chee rang from Telok Anson to know if you had arrived home safely. That was some two weeks ago," he said, looking hard at me.

"Oh, did he? I stopped in Malacca to visit an old school friend there and we had an adventure or two." I said no more. If I were to tell him that during that time, I had met two 'were tigers', fought witches in Bengal and Tibet, demolished the Ark of the Covenant and killed at least twenty men, he would have had me hospitalised for sure.

"How are our racehorses doing?" I asked changing the subject. He appeared pleased and gave me an account of how the races went. "We had two winners this past week, Contract and Siam Rice."

"What about Rice King?"

"Nah, he is only good for polo. No bloody use, a waste of time and money."

I left it at that and went inside with him. My father had eleven racehorses to his name, and to ask him more would keep us out in the blazing sun far too long as each of his horses had his own story.

The aftermath of the War had left my Father a rich but broken man. He was a prisoner of war, our prisoner, my prisoner in my past life, when I was Captain Ichiro Sato of the Imperial Japanese Army. While I was battling the British Army in Burma and then in Kohima, he was languishing in a Kempetai prison in Singapore. The daily beatings and torture made him forget his training in medicine.

Unable to work as a doctor, he tried his hand at general contracting and secured various projects in the rebuilding of post-war Singapore.

Little did I expect to be reborn as his son. How strange, the cycle of Life spun by the mad hands of Destiny.

Of course, even as a child, I had a vague idea as to how he got those scars on his shins but decided not to ask him more about them, as I would have had a lot of explaining to do. I had to keep that a secret. Once I did point to his shins and asked him, in an innocent sort of way, but he smiled, said nothing, and just patted me on the head.

Now that I had almost recovered the memory of my past life as a Japanese soldier, I finally understood how he had got them. It was a form of torture used by the Kempetai, the Japanese Secret Police. They must have poured burning tar on his legs as part of their interrogation.

My father of this life, dressed in his shorts, his scars were there for me to see. I knelt at his feet and re-examined them. The pain, the remorse and the sadness that could not be expressed to anyone, even to him, came pouring down on me.

I was like a tear-soaked handkerchief that could only be wrung in the darkness of a night.

He sat there, lit his pipe and looked at his scars. "Well, now you are old enough to know, that was what they did to me—the Japs, the *Kempetai*."

"Do you not feel anger or hatred?" I asked.

"Hah! We were all soldiers out to kill. We lost, and they won. One must take it like a man. It was war. Everyone is born good, don't forget that."

"Yes, I know you have Japanese friends, and some British ones too."

"Well, any old soldier can find a comrade anywhere, in

whatever uniform or rank and in any army."

"How is that?"

"Well, once you have fought and survived a war, you become a real man. Man enough to be ready to put aside differences that brought you to war and know that we all fought for one reason. To stay alive. Only old ladies harbour hatred and pettiness. You should aspire to be a real man one day." He relit his pipe and picked up the newspaper.

In a way, I was relieved to hear him say so. If I could apologise I would, for the whole Japanese Army, but these were things I could not reveal to him or anyone—maybe I would one day.

My mother and grandmother came out to welcome me home, followed by our two servants. Our dog 'Lucky' came out of his kennel, took one look at me and ran off howling into the bushes.

"He must have given you up for dead!" one of them said and we all had a laugh. Unknown to them, dogs can sense anything unnatural. He might have seen a different aura around me or sensed the pulsing of my keris, Kyai Aweng, in my kitbag.

"I feel I must have died a thousand times coming home," I joked. My grandmother laughed and the others joined in. She wasn't wearing her dentures that day, what with the excitement of my homecoming. At the sight of her toothless mouth, we all laughed even harder.

Chapter Two

My room was the same as I had left it so many months earlier—my desk tidied with books and files arranged in neat piles. With the door closed, I opened the top drawer. Yes, Fat Aunt's red parcel was still there. The three nails, the red string around that snow white pigtail of hair and the small pile of paper charms.

That done, I unpacked my kit bag and took out Kyai Aweng. I could sense its vibration inside the sheath, like a bee trapped in an envelope. Trouble must be brewing somewhere, I thought to myself. Though I was safely home, I felt a sense of foreboding. *Something of danger is on its way, but what and where from?*

Days passed; with my exam results still undelivered, I began to grow restless. One morning, I decided to pay Fat Aunt a visit. Rashid, the chauffeur, would know where she lived with her daughter. "Pagoda Street, on the second floor of that three-storey building." Rashid announced confidently. "That street is one of the most haunted ones in Singapore," he added.

"Will you take me there anyway? Why is it so haunted?" I added.

"That's where the Japanese tortured and killed a lot of the Chinese," he said.

The Japanese again, I thought to myself. Were we that cruel as a race?

The memory of another war surfaced suddenly as my thoughts were interrupted by the screaming and roars from the battle at Sekigahara in 16th century Japan; the memory of that event was stored in my being or my soul for the last four hundred years.

Fat Aunt could not wait to embrace me when I came up the stairs. "Ah Jan! Ah Jan, welcome!" There were tears in her eyes and mine as she hugged me with those fat and flabby arms.

We looked at each other and laughed. "You haven't changed, Fat Aunt!" I said

"But you have grown taller, Ah Jan. I heard about your adventures with Pak Samad. I am proud of you. It is a pity that I could not be there to see you doing your bit for us. It would make me even prouder, my very own student," she beamed.

"Come in, there is no one at home except us." Opening the door wide, I saw an elaborate Chinese shrine for Guan Kong, the God of War, facing the door; otherwise the furnishings were sparse but clean. A sharma or Chinese magpie sang from its cage as we entered.

"See, even the bird welcomes you; have some tea?"

I related my adventures to her in some detail. She was most interested in my getting married to Sri. "You must realise, Ah Jan, those are not man-woman marriages. They are just symbolic ones. Sri is ageless and belongs to the Fairy World. Our worlds cannot mix in the normal way."

"But what about Pak Samad?" I protested.

"He is hundreds of years old and so is Sri. How can you catch up? She married you so as to give you the access to the powers that you need for the tasks allotted. You are under their protection and that should be good enough."

I decided to let Fat Aunt have the last say, but resolved to ask Sri if it was true, that we were "married" only in a symbolic sense. Is she in love with me at all? The Sharma sang louder as though to tease me: "get a hold of yourself, you lovesick cow!"

"Your love life aside," said Fat Aunt now looking serious, "are you aware that your family is in danger? Danger is approaching! Call me if you can't handle the matter yourself," she said cryptically, as I took my leave.

Danger? What kind? I asked myself.

The streets were packed that day with people of all races and colours hurrying somewhere. Rashid drove slowly through the crowd. Some were shouting and waving at us as we passed; others were desperately clamouring to get away, even pushing the slower people aside in order to escape.

"Roll up the windows," Rashid shouted. "Trouble ahead"

"What kind of trouble?" I asked.

"Race riots!"

A man was being set upon by a crowd of knife-wielding thugs. He was stabbed repeatedly and was bleeding everywhere.

"Take that side road!" I ordered Rashid. "Then swing into that lane and we should be home soon."

Rashid did as he was told. As our car passed the bleeding man, I noticed that he looked familiar. He gave me a wink and a smile as we passed.

"Ah, Rashid, don't worry, he will be fine. I know him. It's all an illusion. He will disappear in a minute and return again all healed," I said laughingly.

"Whatever do you mean Ah Jan? Are you sure you know him?" he said glancing at me strangely, while stepping on the accelerator.

We were a bit late reaching home as the first rock was thrown through my bedroom window.

Chapter Three

A group of twelve men had gathered outside our garden fence."Capitalist dog! Show yourself!" they shouted in unison as they hurled more stones at the house. I could hear the glass break and the screams of Ah Mui, one of our servants.

"Rashid, park the car here, beside the kerb!" I yelled, as I ran towards the angry men.

I could not afford to shed blood, so close to home nor was I able to tackle empty-handed all twelve men at once. The nearest three aimed their stones at me, but, luckily, all three missed and that gave me the chance to close in.

Delivering a kick to the groin of the man in the middle, I landed a right to the man on my left, also flooring him. Then turning to block a punch from the man on my right, I kicked him in his right knee. There was a loud click as he went down screaming with pain, then with profanities. The remaining men charged in my direction. Looking back at Rashid, I could see that he had run back to the house to check on the women within.

With no one watching, and the avenue completely deserted except for those thugs, I realised that the chance had come to display my powers. Slipping into Hari Kong, I disappeared from their view.

The men just stood there scratching their heads and wondering where I could have gone. I emerged from behind, snatched two by the scruff of their necks and pulled them in with me into our Eighth Day and left them there, bewildered and shouting in the dark. I repeated the action again and again. In all, I whisked seven men into our Eighth Day, while the remaining five ran for their lives.

Let them stew in Hari Kong for a while, I said to myself, as I emerged into the bright sunlight and walked back to the house to survey the damage.

I suppose it was more the fright than the broken windows that had all the women trembling. Rashid was there helping with the cleaning up.

"Where are all those men?" he looked up at me.

"They all disappeared suddenly," I replied. "They ran away."

I kept those seven men in the dark of Hari Kong for three days and when I went to release them, they were reduced to a bunch of whimpering apes, just happy to see me. I had a good laugh, and warned them to behave, as they grovelled at my feet begging for pardon. “Baka-jin! —mad fellows!” I shouted before throwing them out of the Black Curtains. I knew they would not be throwing stones for a while.

Not long after that event, with my family safe and asleep in the dead of the night, I decided to visit Sri and Pak Samad. I stood in the dark of the garden and waited for an on-coming Grey Wind. Grey Winds tend to avoid crowded cities, so it was past midnight before I spotted one coming my way.

We moved up the Peninsula and I got off at the foot of the Gunong Ledang or Mt. Ophir where the Fairy Folks dwell. Tracing my way through the jungle, I found the megalith. It was full moon and yet I could not see the fog or mists flowing under the rock. Strange that, for once, the rock was not floating in the air as I would have expected it to.

The silence was deafening; except for the gentle breeze rustling leaves overhead, there wasn’t a sound to be heard. I moved across the face of the rock to its edge where the entrance to the Fairy World used to be, but only found a crack in the rock wall.

What has happened, I asked myself, as I stood alone in the dark when there should have been music and laughter, song and dance from the Orang Bunyian or the Invisible Fairy Folks. They were nowhere to be seen.

Unable to control myself I took out Kyai Aweng, my keris, made a slit in the dark and entered Hari Kong.

Perhaps someone there can enlighten me as to where they have all gone, and if they are gone, why did nobody tell me?

"Ah, Jepun!" a familiar voice greeted me. "We have been expecting you!" he laughed.

After a while, I became accustomed to the dark and saw it was Datok, the ancient Chief whom Pat Samad had been talking to when I was first brought into Hari Kong.

"Love sick young man, eh?" he asked. I had to admit that I was. And that I was young in front of Datok's ancient eyes. Now that I knew I had been at the Battle of Sekigahara in the Muromachi Period of Japan (which Pak Samad had told me), I knew my soul must be five hundred years old, but this man looked to be thousands of years older than I.

As though reading my thoughts, he laughed. "No, Jepun, only your memory is younger than mine. We are all of the same age. The older the memory, the older we are. Age is just memory, you are as old as you can look back. You are looking for Sri and Pak Samad?"

"Yes, where are they, Datok? The Rock is not floating anymore, it's just like an ordinary rock," I complained.

"When nobody is home, there is no light in the house, am I right? The whole lot of them have gone to the Southern Ocean at the invitation of Ratu Kidul, Queen of the Southern Seas. These Fairy Folks love to travel to banquets and other festivals, these Fairy Folks of yours," he added smilingly.

"What should I do? Wait for them here or follow on?" I asked, feeling quite helpless.

"You can't join them for you were not invited by Ratu Kidul. She has yet to learn of your existence, maybe next time."

Ratu Kidul is our mythological Queen of the Southern Seas, who lives below the waves of the Indian Ocean. She is often thought to be an ally of the Kingdom of Surakata in Central Java or a Protector of the Javanese people in general.

"Have you been there yourself, Datok?"

"No, I've only been as far as the shores of Java, to watch the procession of our Fairy Folks as they enter the waves and disappear under the ocean. You should see that sometime, or maybe if you are lucky, you might follow them on their next trip. It is a beautiful sight to behold, all the richly dressed people in gold and emeralds, with their gongs and gamelans, their yellow umbrellas going into the sea on a moonlit night. What a spectacle!"

I felt that the Datok took pleasure in describing the Royal retinue just to make me jealous. I laughed at his mischief.

"Next time Datok, I will be leading the delegation into the waves," I said with some confidence.

"Hah, next time maybe a big shark will be there to welcome you!"

Whatever, even with my Sri and Pak Samad absent, I felt happy to be in Hari Kong. I told the Datok of the riots in Singapore and the imprisonment of the seven men in our realm. He nodded, but cautioned me about locking mere mortals in our Eighth Day. "They may die of shock and we don't want ghosts roving in Hari Kong, do we?"

"No, we have enough of them roaming the Earth," I replied.

"We have enough trouble dealing with the living ones, who needs more trouble?" he offered.

"Stay awhile, I will let you meet some more of our people here, then you must return to Japan and find closure to your recent past life before you can move on. How can a man sleep well with every door open?" the Wise One added.

Chapter Four

May 1970—it would be Springtime in Japan, and I found myself increasingly restless and curious about my past life. Fat Aunt's Master, the old Mau San, had told me years ago that my wife Kumiko was still alive in Japan. *How is she now? Is she still alive and waiting there for me?*

A few nights later, while strolling with Nosey and Johnny along the beach in Changi, I spotted a Grey Wind coming our way.

"Eh, do you want to see me disappear?" I asked them.

"Hah! enough of your bloody magic. The last time you showed us your version of magic, our friend Ramasamy suffered a broken nose and was deaf for a few months after you bashed the daylights out of him!" Nosey scolded.

"Stop talking like a madman and try to see if there are any pretty girls around that we can make friends with," said his brother Johnny.

"This time it's for real, okay? Just watch!"

I made a grab for the Grey Wind and rose up in the air. Nosey and Johnny watched me, their mouths opened wider than their eyes before they ran screaming for others to see the sight. By then, I was well away.

I performed this disappearing act, as a way of saying a Sayonara to the people who knew me. Never would I be treated the same by them in this life of mine, not that I wanted that. I had things to do, in this life and my past one. I wanted to make atonements for my deeds of the past, before I could proceed to handle what awaited me in the future. I had to say goodbye to my childhood friends in order to move on.

My parents had long ago given up hope that I was normal, and accepted me for what I was—some kind of a Being that became their son. Not many a year-old infant could conduct an adult conversation with his seniors in three different languages, and not many could predict events to come. They may have initially considered me a freak, then a genius, and later probably a madman, but whatever, I knew that they were still proud that I was their son.

Who cares what the rest of them think of me, I thought, as I searched for another Grey Wind that would take me Northwards as the one I was riding was heading South towards Indonesia.

Sometime over the Riau Islands, a large Grey Wind came my

way. As it approached, I could see that there were many riders along its flanks; most of them were dressed as Javanese or Bugis while two were in Saffron robes of Buddhist monks. None spoke as I jumped on their Wind.

One nodded in acknowledgement and smiled. "Where to?" he finally asked me in Javanese.

"'*nak Kembali ka Negeri Jepun*—going back to Japan," I answered.

He looked at me, then looked at me again, stripping me of my present form, and saw who I had been in the past and laughed.

"*Baik lah, ada masa lagi*—good, there is still time," he said, before he moved up higher in the Wind.

I could sense that I was amongst good people, probably with the same mission as I had—to put down as much Evil as possible, so as to render the Good and Evil of the world on a more even keel. Much like troops on a landing craft heading towards shore, we were each with our own thoughts as to what we would have to do when we went into battle.

The first mystic to get off the Wind was a Javanese warrior. "*Patani, Kelantan!*" he announced.

From what I knew, Patani, on the Malaysian–Thai border was a hotbed of black magic. Perhaps he had been chosen to neutralise the powers of a few, I could only surmise.

The two Buddhist monks left us as we passed over Ayuthiya,

the capital of old Thailand or Siam before the Burmese sacked it in the 18th century. "*Kapban! Kapban!*—just going home!" they announced. Their solemn faces, now breaking into generous smiles as they waved their palm leaf fans at us in parting. Whether you are a monk or monkey, home is where one finds or feels a sense of belonging.

How I envied them, even monks whose home was the sacred confines of a cold, white marble temple. By contrast, my heart, my soul was scattered in three different places, each of which I could only afford a minimum of attachment.

I began to recall what Pak Samad, my teacher, once said: "The more you know of your past, the less you can do in your present, and much less can you do in the future."

How lucky mere mortals are, only equipped to live one life at a time, I mused.

That gave me the resolve to settle all matters in my past so as to return to the now and be ready for the future.

Would my past be there? Could I now close that chapter?

"*Ada masa lagi*—there is still time" was what the Javanese mystic had said, and with that hope in my mind, I aimed the Grey Wind towards the Land of the Rising Sun.

Chapter Five

With little memory of my past life, save my name as Captain Ichiro Sato of the 138th Regiment, I had very little to go on to find my former wife Kumiko in Japan. As the wind moved up north towards the Homeland, I began to devise a way of tracing my way home.

The Yasukuni Shrine is where all Japanese War Dead are enshrined; some two and a half million names are listed there as Kami or Holy Spirits, who gave their lives for the Emperor and country. It was built by the Meiji Emperor in the late 19th century to commemorate the war dead, and names had been added after each civil or international conflict that Japan had been involved in until the end of the Second World War.

Located in the Chiyoda district of Tokyo, it would be visited by many war veterans and their families; thus, I considered it might be a good place to find someone whom I had once known.

I landed on the grounds just outside the Chumon Torii sometime in the night. The gates were already closed and just a few people were to be seen, all hurrying home.

I waited in Hari Kong till dawn broke to display the pink and white glory of the Sakura or cherry blossoms. My heart felt heavy at the sight. *How transient is a lifetime and how frail the flight of a loose petal. How far further can a fallen blossom fall?* Sadness filled my soul when I thought of my fallen comrades in Burma.

I looked around and saw a policeman walking towards the gate. He was in his thirties. Copying his features in my mind, but with a more weathered look and a head of white hair, I transformed myself into an older version of him, maybe a lookalike of his grandfather, and then I emerged out of Hari Kong.

May in Tokyo is always wonderful. The soft sunlight filtered through the pines and maple as I walked along the causeway towards the Haiden where visitors are allowed to go and pray.

I had been there before, probably thirty years earlier when we set out to conquer South East Asia. The shouts of '*Banzai!*' came back to me as I looked at the well-kept grounds of the shrine. I looked to the Daichi Torii or the First gateway and then to the Daiini Torii, the gates of hinoki cypress wood with its Sixteenth Petalled Chrysanthemum Mon or Emblem of the Emperor.

Little had changed and yet much had. Absent was the anxiety

and gravitas of our first visit—the whole nation was anxious when the prospect of a Great Asiatic War was just over the horizon.

The atmosphere had been replaced by the din of Tokyo's modern traffic and the peaceful reflection of the morning sun from well-polished glass of the multi-storied buildings.

Visitors to the shrine had begun to arrive. I strained to see if I could recognise a face or two of any still-living comrades.

Most of the visitors that morning were women, still wearing their kimonos and carrying their little parasols. They made a beautiful picture, what with those cherry blossoms and pine trees lining the causeway. I knew that Hiroshige would be glad to make a woodblock print of the scene that I was witnessing. If only I could make Time stand still, but Time flows on and unfolds even greater surprises to the beholder.

So, as the white-haired gentleman that I had transformed myself into, I stood under the Chumon Torii, the last gate before the Haiden, smiling at all visitors as they passed. Only a few returned my bows, as most had their sights set on the main hall, the Haiden, to pray for the departed souls. There were plenty of elderly gentlemen around, most were leftovers from the War—scarred or scared into worlds of their own, some labelled senile and some simply called mad.

Whatever, I persevered, looking into every old face for

someone I might still recognise. Sometime in the afternoon, a man in his fifties approached the Torii. He looked familiar, even after all these years.

"*Okano san!*" I cried.

He stopped, bowed and looked hard at me: "Do we know each other?"

"I am Captain Ichiro Sato, do you not remember?" I chanced.

His face turned pale, while he surveyed my features. "How we have aged," he said, bowing politely. "I thought you were 'lost' in Burma."

"I thought we were all lost in Burma," I helped him on.

"How is Kumiko? Are you still living in Saitama ken?"

What a lucky break! It was worth the wait.

"Someday you must come and visit us," I said. "In fact, why don't we go to my house today? After all, Saitama is only less than an hour away, there is so much that I want to ask you."

Okano agreed, and we walked to the Ichigaya station with him leading the way. He paid our fares while I tried fumbling for my wallet.

"Small change, leave it to me" he said. I thanked him as we found two empty seats, which was rare on a Tokyo subway.

"So, what have you been doing since the War?" I inquired.

"I had been lucky, Sato sama. When I was repatriated from Burma, I came home to our fishing village in Sendai. There I married Marumi, whose father owned the local Sake brewery. I must say that the Kami have been kind to me and my family. What about you Ichiro?" he asked.

"Well, I have been travelling the Earth, trying to find myself" I half lied.

Okano nodded in understanding. "After the War, so many of us just lost the will to live and so many their lives. It had been difficult to live in defeat, but still, our enemy the Americans stayed to help us rebuild. It took two hands to clap, two parties to enjoin a war, and two parties to make peace," he concluded.

I stayed silent as our train pulled into the station.

"Can you still remember the way to our house?" I challenged him. "Of course! how can we forget all those midnight sake parties at your home? And your lovely *oksan*, your wife Kumiko? Is she still as beautiful?" he asked.

"Well, I will let you be the judge" I said, allowing him to lead the way.

As we walked towards Sakado, the place became more and more familiar. Though very much rebuilt after the war, the laneways remained the same and that Ryokan owned by Mrs. Osada was still there.

We turned left together, Okano never suspected a thing as I was confident enough to point to the lane where my house would be.

"Okano–san, would you go ahead first, Kumiko will be there, while I just nip over to that little shop and get us some sake and titbits?"

"Why don't we go together?" he protested.

"No, no. Give Kumiko a surprise and tell her that I will be back in a minute. That will give you both time to catch up on the past." He reluctantly agreed and I was able to walk away while he went towards the door.

Out of his sight, I managed to slip back into Hari Kong. I had never been so excited, my heart was almost bursting in my chest and I could hardly breathe.

Okano-san knocked on the door. I could hear footsteps and the click as the door slid open.

"*Hai!*" came the sound of a young woman, hurriedly wiping her wet hands on the apron and bowing low.

"*Michiko–san ka?*" Okano asked.

Michiko? Who is Michiko? Do I have a daughter?

Chapter Six

I could only watch from the Realm of the Eighth Day, invisible, yet unable to affect the outcome. I was at my wits end as to how I could salvage this situation.

Here was an old friend and a comrade in arms, Okano, in front of my house, ready to tell the daughter I never knew I had, about meeting me, her dead father, at the Yasukuni Shrine!

"Ah, I am Okano, your father's old friend. We were at the Yasukuni Shrine and we decided to come back here to see Kumiko san, your mother. Michiko san, how well you have grown!" Okano said. "You were only a little baby in your mother's arms when I last saw you."

So far so good, I told myself. Fate be good, I prayed.

Michiko bowed low and kneeled to take Okano's sandals.

God! What's next? I thought in desperation,

Just then, as Fate would have it, two fighting tomcats fell

from the low roof and onto Okano's back as he stooped to take off his sandals. One of them, still wild with fury scratched at Okano's neck and right ear before tearing off down the lane with the other cat following in hot pursuit.

"*Tomi san! Tomi san!*" Michiko screamed after the second cat, at the same time helping Okano up to his feet.

"*O sumimasen, dozo sumimasen!*", Michiko, now in tears, kneeled at Okano's feet in apology.

"It is alright, it is alright," he replied, trying to staunch the flow of blood from his neck and ear.

A neighbour came out to help and, seeing the bleeding Okano, suggested that he needed to be seen urgently by a doctor. "My car is parked just behind the house, please follow me," he offered as he helped Okano along.

Okano looked back at the distraught Michiko. "Don't worry, I will visit again. I am sorry for this upset. Tell your father that we will meet at the Yasukuni at some other time, and please apologise to your mother." Michiko, not knowing what he meant could only whisper more words in apology as they left.

I heaved a sigh of relief. Saved, by two tomcats! What luck!

Still in Hari Kong, I went in to my old house to look around. Nothing much had changed; my family lived frugally as prescribed by the Code of Bushido and the Hojo Soun of the Samurai. I could see that Kumiko or my daughter Michiko had hung a new scroll in the tokonoma or recessed alcove in the room.

Our family's treasure, the Daisho, should be on the kake stand. Those two swords had been my great-grandfather's when he was a Samurai serving the Sakai Clan many years before. With sadness, I could see only the wakizashi, the shorter sword. I had taken the long sword to the War with me. It was also the same sword used by the Burmese villagers to kill me with while I slept. As these memories came over me, I was overwhelmed with feelings of sadness, anger and confusion.

Looking around I finally saw my old self, Captain Ichiro Sato, on a framed black and white photo on the wall. Taken while in uniform, with my white gloves in one hand and my sword in the other, I looked quite well in that life.

On the table were two framed photographs, both taken on our wedding day. Kumiko—beautiful and striking in her bridal kimono, and I—in my traditional best, sporting the two Sakai Mons or Crests on the front of the kataginu or jacket of the kamishimo, the traditional dress of the samurai. The other showed me in my uniform as a Japanese Officer standing behind my pretty bride, taken a few weeks before I was sent to the war.

There was no sign of Kumiko. Her bed was made and her little boxes of make-up placed neatly beside the dressing mirror. A vase with only a stalk of cherry blossom was on her table.

I could detect a faint smell of her perfume, or maybe it was Michiko's?

The phone rang and Michiko answered. "*Moshi moshi, hai, hai*—I will be there soon, please tell my mother I will be there soon. Thank you very much," and she hung up.

She looked flustered after the incident of the tomcats and Okano, as she packed some clothes and a new tube of toothpaste in her bag.

"I'll be late, I'll be late," she muttered to herself.

Michiko should be around twenty six years old, I surmised. She must have been born while I was away fighting our war. Now an adult and looking very much like her mother, I felt pleased at seeing her independence and composure.

On a rack, I saw a coat that sported a company's logo, "Mitsui Bank", and her name tag clipped on its lapel. She should be well-looked after as a bank employee.

Still in Hari Kong, I followed her out of the house as she hurried back to the Shin toshin station. She caught a train going north and some five stops away, she got off and hurried out taking the second road left. It did not take her long to reach the hospital and find her mother's ward. *So, Kumiko is ill?*

"Ah, Michiko san, your mother is waiting, she has not long, you'd better be quick," said a nurse on the corridor. Bowing low and keeping her composure, Michiko turned and went into the room.

Kumiko, looking drawn and pale, was happy to see her. “Michiko, I am happy that you have come. I know I haven’t long left,” she said, her voice barely audible.

“Please, don’t say such things. You will get better and we will watch the cherry blossoms of next Spring.”

Kumiko smiled and looked down. “Let’s hope so,” she said, shaking her head ever so gently, “let’s hope so.”

So, this was Kumiko, the pretty girl I had married before going to war, and this young girl was my daughter. If only I could emerge out of Hari Kong and announce that I was not dead and hold them in my arms. But one can’t live a life backwards—Heaven has its rules, and Time—though stretchable—is on a forward march. Advanced Mystics can reverse time, a feat I had seen Aweh do, but he had not yet taught me. I had never felt so helpless in my life, yet I was relieved to realise that I could never again be what I had once been. Aweh had his reasons for not teaching me then.

I stayed and allowed the two ladies time to themselves. I had been away from them for a lifetime, and as such, I felt that I had no right to their lives and their secrets at this stage.

When it was time for Michiko to leave, I stayed in the room with Kumiko. I could see that she was very ill and, though still beautiful, her body was thin and frail. Her breathing became heavy after a short time. I decided it was time and I came out of

Hari Kong, looking like my old self, resplendent in my uniform as Captain Ichiro Sato .

" Kumiko, I am here," I whispered .

Her eyes opened wider now but too weary to be shocked. She smiled and stretched out her thin hand. "I knew we would meet again Ichiro. I see you in my dreams, every night."

Tears from another lifetime welled up in my eyes. I could see that she too was crying as she clutched my hand.

" Please Ichiro, *anata*, do not leave me again," she said weakly, "take me with you."

I nodded before her hand slipped out of mine. Closing her eyes, she smiled as she slowly sank away.

Maintaining my form as her Ichiro, I stayed in the room for a while to let her see me as she left this the world of Man. I prayed for her passage to the Other World and wished her a better birth in time to come.

The sadness remaining in my heart gradually lifted as I left her room. Outside the sun was shining after the light rain. It was time to catch another Grey Wind.

Chapter Seven

I had not long to wait when the Wind came, almost on purpose, to collect me. Latching on its flank, we moved over the built up areas of Saitama. So many people, all living the life of ants, I mused, as we roared southwards over Tokyo Bay and over the Pacific and beyond.

The sun had already set and stars had become visible, one by one as though the Guardian of Night had flicked on the many light switches in the sky.

I decided to climb higher in the Wind as it swept along the waves. "Meow! Meow!" the sound of a cat and laughter from above met me. "Si Jan! Was that good or what? Meow!......... Meow!"

"Who's that?" I shouted.

"*Siapa lagi?*—who else?" The voice sounded familiar.

"Aweh? Is it you?" I shouted back in surprise. "Is that you?"

"*Siapa lagi?* Who else would help you, Jepun!" came his reply and laughter.

Aweh, my old companion who had left me to fight my own battles after our adventures in Bangla Desh, was back! I was overjoyed to say the least.

"Do you have the keris, Kyai Aweng, that I made for you?" he shouted down.

"Here!" When I reached him, the old warrior gave me a hug with his free hand. He had not changed. His flowing hair kept neat by a red headband, his ancient costume of an old Malay warrior was unchanged.

"Where have you been?" I asked.

"Siberia! Where else?" he said. I had to learn more from the people there, the Siberian Shamans. Si Jan, you have to keep improving yourself as you go. What you have learnt has just set you on the beginning of the Mystic Path. You have to acquire more Power, so as to face the bigger and bigger challenges that will be thrown at you," he added.

I knew he had spoken the truth, with what I knew or had learnt so far, I was just a novice in their eyes.

"Will you teach me more?" I asked.

"What do you think I am here for?" he answered with a question.

Nothing had changed, Aweh always answered a question

with another.

Looking at me again, he threw his head back and laughed. "That was good with the two fighting tomcats, wasn't it? I saved you just in time."

"Was it you who helped me when Okano met my daughter?"

"*Siapa lagi?*—who else?" We both laughed. "What a close shave," I said, "imagine if Okano got to tell my daughter that he had met me in the Yasukuni Shrine!"

"Yes, your daughter would have thrown him out of the house!" quipped Aweh.

"Meow! Meow! Thank God for the tomcats!" We shared a good laugh as the Wind moved us on.

"Where to?"

"Where else? Papua New Guinea. Have you tasted human flesh?" he asked in return.

"No. Have you?"

"No, they have. And if you are not careful, they will eat you too. Are you afraid?"

I shook my head.

"I watched as you pulled the seven rascals into Hari Kong the other day those guys who threw stones at your father's house. You can't just pull all your enemies into our Hari Kong, Jepun. You must learn how to tackle ten or even twenty men all at once. You have to acquire better skills in unarmed combat."

"Who will teach me?"

"Ask your Uncle Chan when you get back, he will be the one. You need a real Master, a real Sifu, Jepun."

Uncle Chan? When Nosey went to Uncle Chan to learn Kung Fu many years ago, all he did was make Nosey throw stones along the railway track from one spot to the other, and then throw them back to their original spot at the end of each lesson.

He kept at Nosey for a year until the mere mention of Uncle Chan's name would make Nosey cringe, close his eyes and shake his hand in the air and shout "never again!"

"*Our* Uncle Chan?" I asked Aweh in disbelief.

Aweh cringed, closed his eyes, shook his hand wildly and stuck out his tongue."

Wheeak! *That* Uncle Chan!" laughing his head off.

He had read my mind and seen my thoughts, the bloody rascal.

One day, I will learn how to read minds and see thoughts. I will learn how to conjure up two fighting tomcats, and make and mould red hot iron into kerises with my bare hands. One day, I will be like you, Aweh.

Aweh looked at me and smiled. "Perhaps, perhaps, one day you will be better than Aweh, Jepun! But first, we will go down to Papua to meet some cannibals. You're coming, aren't you?"

What else was there for me to do? Except to be eaten by a few hungry cannibals?

"Of course! Of course! I'm dying to come."

Chapter Eight

We sailed with the Grey Wind down the home islands towards the Philippines and down towards the Indonesian Island Archipelago and made a slight detour or swing to pass over the island of Java. I knew that Aweh did so just to please me.

Was my lovesickness over Sri so apparent? Ah, but then Aweh reads minds and he could see that I had just closed the chapter on my last life as Ichiro Sato, and that now it should be a new beginning.

"We'll watch our folks return from Ratu Kidul's feast," he said, as we slowed the Wind over the southern shores of Java. "Look down!" Aweh pointed below.

As we hovered over the site, we could see a greenish glow on the ocean that was gradually moving towards the shore.

"Watch closely, they won't be long!"

True to form, the flag bearers emerged from the waves, followed by the musicians with their flutes, drums and gongs. The gamelan players were lugging their heavy brass bowls, and the whole band was playing a strange tune as emerged from the sea.

Next came the large Yellow Parasol bearers signifying the presence of Royalty and then we could see the Fairy Princess from Gunong Ledang, Pak Samad and then Sri. The Royal retinue was followed by about fifty retainers of sorts, of warriors and camp followers.

They were all dressed in their best, and as predicted by the Datok, in gold studded with emeralds over costumes of the finest silk.

The most remarkable sight was that they all emerged from the ocean bone dry.

Pak Samad and Sri sensed that we were around, looked up at us, and waved. Pak Samad shouted: "Go on with your task, and we will see you two soon!" Sri just smiled as she waved.

My heart felt heavy at the sight of her slowly fading from view as the entourage went on its way. Aweh, sensing my heartache, placed his hand on my shoulder. "Jepun, a real man must be able to pick up something he loves and let go of it when the time comes, without regret or remorse. You must exercise detachment, Jepun. You will be here for a lifetime, with only one lifetime's share of hurt and sorrow. You should have pity on Sri, someone who lives forever, always losing anything or anyone she loves to Time. However long that Time can be stretched, a mere mortal will not outlast his time, unless you become one of us."

"Aweh, can I?"

"Well, you did marry Sri, even though that was to help you acquire the Powers you needed for the tasks ahead. It would be perhaps possible for you to join the Fairy Folk if you had consummated the marriage with Sri. Do you know what that is?" Aweh laughed, knowing fully well that I was still a virgin.

"I have a fair idea," I said. I had seen a 'blue movie' once that Nosey and Johnny showed me the night before my exams to distract me.

"Rascals!" said Aweh, "but you should realise by now that you were born to operate on a different plane than the Noseys and Johnnys of this world. Whether you study or not, your life will fall into place as preordained. Whether you work or stay in bed, food will come to you. You will have everything you will ever need in proportion—just enough and not more. You have taken a vow as a Mau San, a Chinese mystic, and like all real mystics, you will never be rich or too poor."

"So is it worthwhile to become one of your Fairy Folk?" I asked him.

Aweh stroked his moustache, and with that faraway look,

replied: "Isn't everything preordained?"

"Come! Jepun, we have to move on"

"Aweh, what's this 'task' with the cannibals?" I asked as the Wind picked up and moved us towards Papua New Guinea.

"You will know pretty soon," he replied as we moved higher. Monsoon clouds were ahead and we could see streaks of lightning and then the rain and thunder.

"Si Jan," Aweh said, still with that distant look, "we are going to a land of the First People. They are the descendants of the Earlier Race of Men. They have not changed their ways and cannibalism is just one of them. They have various 'Power Objects' that we require for the battle that is soon to come."

"What kind of objects?" I asked, hanging on to the flanks of the wind and drenched by the onslaught of a real tropical downpour. I could hardly see Aweh, though he was no more than a foot away.

"'Stones of Power' that they treasure and now use for their evil ends," Aweh continued, "when the Star People came to Earth, they left these Power Objects with the First People, along with teachings on how to use them for the benefit of Mankind. But sadly, those teachings were never written down, instead they were transmitted through oral teachings, from one witch doctor or holy man to the next."

"So, what happened?"

“What happened?” Aweh laughed. “Being cannibals, they ate their last holy man, they even ate his brains thinking that his teachings would stay with them. Well, all they got was a bout of indigestion and probably the runs, so they started making up their own crazy rituals—those blood sacrifices of pigs and captured enemies, hoping to invoke a power of some kind.

“They still have those stones, but have no idea of how to use them for their own benefit or for Mankind’s. We have to get them before the Evil Ones get their hands on them, otherwise Si Jan, all will be lost!” Aweh sounded serious as he finished his last sentence. There were more flashes of lightning ahead as we moved on.

A grey and brown being flew past us screaming into the storm.

“What was that?” I yelled.

“One of their witch doctors!” Aweh replied, “they have mastered some powers, mostly from the Evil Ones.”

“Are they dangerous?”

“You will know soon enough,” came his reply. “ When we are down there,” he continued, pointing to the middle of the island, “try not to sleep!”

Chapter Nine

"*Anyang Baling Katimu!*" Aweh shouted to the Grey Wind as we hovered over the Sepik River. "Land of the Asmat! Headhunters and cannibals!" he whispered with a smile. "Have no worry, Jepun, you are invulnerable!"

Despite being so near the equator, Papua New Guinea was cold, wet and humid when we landed. We made our way down the slippery slope of well-churned mud holding on to the giant yam stalks and any branch that we could get a grip on.

"Aweh, why not go into Hari Kong and save ourselves this mess?" I asked.

"It is not safe, as they can be waiting there for us—it is better to battle them in broad daylight and on solid ground. Be careful!"

Before we could go any further, the sound of the Tom-tom drums could be heard further down the slope.

"We have been spotted, Jepun. Get ready!" Aweh shouted as

the first wave of arrows flew towards us.

"*Halimunan!* Be invisible!" he ordered.

Fat Aunt's teaching of the Mau San art of disappearing came into use now. With three claps of my hand after invoking the Powers, I entered this zone of brick-coloured pink and stayed there. This was my second time disappearing the Mau San way after that clumsy attempt from Chee's house in Telok Anson—I nearly died then so I was more careful this time.

Aweh was nowhere to be seen as I headed down the ravine towards the cluster of palm thatched huts and the war cries from a bunch of scantily clad dark natives. Many sported feather decorations in their hair and pig tusks or porcupine quills through their big noses.

One had a large oyster shell as his chest piece hanging from his neck and red war paint on his face. He looked menacing, but he had no idea that I was just standing beside him.

Time for some fun, I thought to myself. They had their arrows stuck on the ground before them ready for use. I borrowed one and still invisible, stabbed it into the behind of this fearsome warrior. He let out an almighty yelp as he was jabbed the second time.

I then moved on to the next warrior doing the same before the whole bunch retreated further down the slope, screaming in fear.

Aweh emerged laughing at my mischief. "That will give them

something to talk about at their next 'Sing Sing' or communal feast.

"So, where is the stone, your Power object?" I asked.

"Here!" pointing to a large boulder, some fifteen feet tall.

"This big thing? How the hell are we going to take it with us?" I asked incredulously.

Aweh laughed as he looked at me. "Jepun! Si Jan! …… watch!"

He slapped the boulder with his right hand and with his left wrote a few symbols on the rock. The giant rock slowly shrank in size and kept on shrinking.

"What the… ?" I could only manage to say before the rock became as small as a brick and then finally as small as a pebble.

Aweh enjoyed at my surprise, while tucking the stone safely into his pocket. "Yes, Jepun you have a lot, a lot more to learn."

"So, that's how the Egyptians Pyramids or Stonehenge were built? By making these Power Stones big again?" I said, trying to be smart.

"What do you think, Jepun?" came his reply.

Chapter Ten

So began another lesson from Aweh. "Everything that you see, be it you or me or the rocks or even mountains around you, is an illusion. Nothing exists in real form unless it wants to be what it is and what you see is what you want to see.

"Like those warriors for an example. They wanted to look fierce, so they painted themselves fierce and became fierce. So if you think they are fierce, they are fierce." He added: "let's walk towards that clump of trees and I'll show you."

I was beginning to see what he was driving at.

"They, the warriors created an illusion. You, Si Jan, being invulnerable would not be afraid of them, now would you?" he asked me.

"No, that was why I was managed to stick a few arrows in their bums," I replied.

"Exactly. That holds true too even for an inanimate object. It has the power to hold a form. So, the boulder became a boulder to you and will remain so … until your power overcomes its determination to keep its present form."

"Something few can do," I interjected.

"Therefore if you can override its energy with yours, you can will it to forget its form and become what you want it to be."

"How is that done?"

"Ah, Si Jan, this is how." Aweh pulled me closer and whispered some sacred words in my ear. "Those are the words you utter to make anything lose its memory. Memory of its intended form. And this," Aweh drew a few sacred symbols in the air as he continued, "is how you make it conform to the shape you want it to be.

"Try it on that tree," Aweh said, pointing to a gnarled tembusu trunk beside us. "First, pat the trunk with your right hand, then say those words and draw the symbols on its trunk as you do with your left hand; it will shrink until you stop patting it."

I had always wanted to do magic—magic of any kind, be it card tricks at a party, or real magic, such as this, beside this Malay warrior who was my teacher and friend.

"Like this?" I asked.

The tree started getting smaller as I did my spell and it only stopped when it became a bonsai.

"Wow! Aweh, this is fun. How do I get it to grow big again?"

"You wanted to build pyramids, didn't you?" Aweh laughed.

"Just do the reverse, stupid."

"How Aweh?"

"Just use your left hand to pat it and your right to draw the signs while repeating the words I have just taught you."

The bonsai started to grow bigger as I did, and before long returned to its original size, that of an old gnarled tembusu tree.

Aweh looked every inch a warrior to me. I felt proud and blessed to be a student of his. There was much to learn from this man. He was ageless and timeless. Humble and unassuming and always giving, I looked at him with the greatest respect. He smiled as he must have read my thoughts

"Jepun! Let's move on!"

Before he could finish, a net of some kind was thrown over us. Aweh and I reached for our weapons, but we felt bound by this net. "Kriyat!" I yelled to summon my invisible spear. It came in a flash, hovered around us but appeared unable to help.

"A Hair Net. Made of human hair. The Evil Ones are here!" Aweh explained.

Kriyat, our spear began circling us as we struggled to get free, but the Hair Net grew tighter and tighter with our every effort.

From the corner of my eye, I could see an elderly man approaching from the darker shades of the trees, followed by a gaggle of those once terrified warriors. With their leader in front, they regained their old composure. Now with red-rimmed eyes glaring, they sensed blood and were ready to kill.

"Kriyat! *Bunuh kan!*" Aweh ordered our spear to kill, but the elderly man—with just a smile and a wave of his hand—made the spear inert and still on the ground. It only quivered as it lay, much like a dying butterfly.

"Be careful Jepun. That's one of them! The Evil Ones! They are only afraid of seawater." said Aweh choking, as the old man suddenly used the spear on him.

"Ha! No more power now!" roared the old man as he stabbied Kriyat deeper into Aweh. Blood gushed first from his chest wound and then from his mouth.

"No more power, Evil One, no more power…." Aweh muttered as his head slumped on his chest and he stopped breathing.

"Take them to the canoe!" the old one commanded. "Our boat is waiting out at sea!"

An Asmat war canoe is a sight to behold. Made of a dugout tree trunk and with an outrigger on each side, it is typically powered by twenty or more armed paddlers all chanting war cries as they go.

This one was festooned with the red leaves of a palm and the yellow strips of a young coconut leaf frond. We were their unwilling cargo, trussed up and secured on the craft's mid-section; we were helpless while under the spell of their Hair Net.

Their leader, now with Kriyat in his hand, gave the signal for us to move. The canoe was swift, paddled by twenty warriors as it sped down the Sepik River towards the sea.

Crowds of tribesmen had gathered along the banks of the Sepik as word travelled that two Magic men had been captured and were soon to be eaten. Some tribes along the way were hostile to our captors, and, although arrows were exchanged as our war canoe sped through, no one was injured.

Before long, we reached the muddy estuary as the Sepik empties out to sea. On all sides mangrove swamps with their resident crocodiles were there to greet the war party.

The old man used Kriyat to point to a two-black-masted schooner or sailing ship in the horizon. It was a Pinisi, a trading schooner favoured by the Bugis pirates.

"Paddle us there!" he shouted and the canoe made a slight adjustment aiming its prow towards the ship.

As it came alongside, four pairs of hands grabbed our net and we were unceremoniously dumped on her bare deck.

The headhunters accepted gifts of salt, a few axe heads and paddled away with their war cries back towards the river mouth.

By then, the sun had begun to set, but before the coming darkness, I was able to take stock of my situation. I was alive and uninjured. Smoking and joking amongst themselves, the evil-looking crew sat around me as the ship took wind and headed out to sea.

Aweh appeared dead; I did try to rouse him with my feet, but he was motionless. In the fading light, however, I could see a slight smile on his face. Was he playing dead? I kept still watching Aweh's lifeless body as we sailed further over the horizon. By the light of the moon, I saw Aweh's eye open and close again and noticed his smile grow wider.

Trapped under this magical Hair Net of the Evil ones, no magic could be performed, but, there might still be a chance. Aweh let out a slight groan as he fell on his side. The crew watched as I pretended to move to sit his body upright. Aweh fell to his side again.

"Leave him alone!" one of the crew ordered. "He is already a dead man."

I pulled at his shirt for just one more try. This time Aweh stayed sitting up as more blood flowed down his chest. Pretending to clean him, I managed to find the pebble.

"No magic under the net?" I asked them as I rubbed it with my left hand, chanted the sacred words and drew the signs with my right. Though under the net, the pebble grew and grew.

"Oi! What are you up to?" the old fellow shouted.

But it was too late. The boulder grew to its former height, then grew even more as I willed it to, tearing the Hair Net away.

Aweh let out a cough and then his old laugh. "Ha! Let's see

what you can do now!" standing up and waving his own keris.

"Kriyat! *Bunuh!*—Kill!" The spear wrenched itself out of the old man's hand and moving over the surprised crew, did its job, and only the old man, the Evil one, was left alive.

He started chanting and as he did, he slowly became less solid as he tried to fade into the Ether. He was beaten by the sudden loud crack and the sound of splintering wood. The boulder, weighing a good few tons now, was too much for the wooden Pinisi as it crashed through her timbers and sea water rushed up to meet us.

As the sea water touched the Evil One's feet, a streak of blue lightning rose to the top of his head. He emitted a bluish glow, then with a soft 'pop', disappeared leaving a smell of rotting meat.

"He's gone, they are gone!" Aweh announced as we clung to the sinking vessel before deciding on the next course of action.

We had not long to wait, for something solid came under our feet, lifting us above water as they moved us away from the fast sinking craft.

"Aweh! What is under our feet?" I yelled.

By the light of the stars, I could vaguely glimpse the shape of two inverted bowls, each very large and long. Then I saw a head with a hawk-like beak emerge from the water.

"Sea turtles!" Aweh shouted. "A gift from Ratu Kidul, Queen

of the Southern Ocean! Si Jan! You will get to meet her now!"

God! Magic boulders, now sea turtles and the Queen of the Southern Ocean! What was next?

Chapter Eleven

We travelled for a while on the backs of these two leatherback turtles. It was clearly an effort for them to keep us afloat on the calm dark sea, but we made slow steady progress.

After about an hour, we neared a patch of water so calm that it reflected the moon on its surface. The turtles surprised us by diving underwater.

"Can you swim Aweh?" I yelled.

Awey threw his head back and laughed: "Who needs to swim?"

A large hole had opened up, much like a swirling vortex of sea water. The two turtles, with us still on their backs, slid down its walls and into the darkness below.

As we neared the bottom, we noticed lights on the walls of water; they grew brighter as we approached what I realised was a structure under the sea.

Two men came forward to greet us. They were well-attired in our ancient costume of a well-woven headgear of Sampin, their baju and pants of the same purple and silver thread cloth, with a black and gold threaded Sampin wrapped around their mid-section and each with our ubiquitous keris tucked in the folds.

They raised their hands in salute: "Welcome to our warriors, our Queen awaits." As they moved aside and showed us the way to the gates, we stepped down from the backs of the two giant leatherbacks and stood on the ground; though wet and much like a drained swimming pool, the water was only at our ankles and was quickly flowing away.

There was no sensation of Time or Space, which was nothing new to me, what with Hari Kong, Grey Winds and Timeless Warriors. But being under the sea and still alive and breathing, that was something very new.

Then, a kind of sunlight shone, lighting up the place as though we were back on a tropical shore only there was no sky above us, only water, only the sea.

I had little time to reflect further as more beings appeared, just as well attired as the last two. With more smiles of welcome, they ushered us into deeper chambers that smelt of freshly gathered seaweed, lit up by lamps that glowed but gave off no heat.

What a place, I thought. Aweh laughed and said "*Banyak*

lagi!—more yet to come!"

Drums and the Gamelans started to play! A full orchestra under the ocean? I couldn't believe my senses—my world was literally turned upside down.

It took me a while to gather myself and realise that this was real and I was not dreaming. When the orchestra stopped, there was a hush and a parting of the crowd to reveal the entrance of a group of warriors carrying spears and amok catchers—fierce weapons, U-shaped with inward pointing barbs made to pinion any mad man to the ground.

"You are not mad yet, are you?" Aweh whispered, sensing my apprehension. "They are only for show, but also to make sure you do not misbehave amongst the ladies."

"What ladies?"

"Look behind you!"

I almost jumped out of my skin when I did and saw an array of the most beautiful beings lined up behind me. I turned, bowed low and saluted them with my folded palms, not knowing which one of them was the Queen. "Do like me," Aweh whispered, as he knelt on one knee before the salutation; I followed suit, aware of the spears and amok-catchers behind me.

"You were brave, Aweh, and you were fast thinking, Si Jan, we enjoyed the spectacle," said the lady in the middle There I was before the Queen of the Southern Ocean, Ratu Kidul, dressed in golden silk and emeralds. Beautiful and ageless, though our Myths made her out to be nearly one thousand years old. She looked at me, read my soul and smiled.

"Your wife, Sri, has told us a lot about you. I will be happy to grant you some of the secrets of Higher Learning that Mankind has lost to the sea. Whatever written wisdom or Powers that were lost in their shipwrecks, their wars, we have them all. You will be taught what we think you need for the moment, but we will also allow you to return for more when the time comes. Do stay with us awhile, let us make you welcome, but we must observe the Rules of the Above and the Below. Pak Samad and Sri will be waiting when you return to Gunong Ledang."

With that, she turned and, with her retinue, moved into the wall of water and was gone.

Still on our knees, I asked Aweh: "Eh, what's this.... Above and Below?"

"*Naskhah, Si Jan, naskhah,* arrangements agreed between the Land and the Sea for the two to exist, side by side without one overwhelming the other. Protocol! Si Jan." Aweh winked. "No misbehaving!"

Chapter Twelve

“This is the Munshi, our translator, our scribe and font of knowledge for whatever else you need to know in the field of Ancient Literature or Ancient Lore,” said one of the Queen’s attendants, pointing to a wizened old man in the corner—a man of darker countenance, with an unhappy scowl and heavy feathery brows that almost shielded his deep set eyes. He gave me a nod and looked down again at his feet and said nothing.

“What would like to know?” he whispered.

I might as well ask him a broad and stupid question.

“What is in India?”

Aweh saw that I was overwhelmed and stepped in: “Show this young man what you have from the Libraries of Alexandria and maybe what you recovered from the Treasure Ships of our Admiral Cheng Ho. Let him choose something to start with.”

“Come with me then,” the Munshi said, turning to his right and passing through the billowing green curtains of damp seaweed.

"Come, *ikut!*" he commanded, when he spotted us still unmoving.

Aweh patted me on the back: "Si Jan, go with the Munshi, ask him about the secrets of Time Travel, of living under water and of Star travel, and whatever else. I know you have been interested in those things since you were young……. yes, I was there, we were there, and watched you horde your comic books under the bed to read by torchlight when the rest were asleep at night," he added.

"You mean you have been watching me since I was nine?"

"What do you think?" Aweh laughed, "we had to know if you were the right one."

The Queen's library was an underwater cave, large enough to contain ten Buckingham Palaces and more. There were stacks and stacks of manuscripts, scrolls and maps, along with a few hundred globes from sunken ships.

"All these things, mankind has lost or thrown away due to ignorance or greed. All these things, we saved so that they would be ready for the New World to come when Man is ready and wise enough to seek them again," the wizened Munshi whispered.

He must have been a librarian before, talking in whispers even in this life. As solemn as an undertaker, I followed him around as he pointed to one stack of books and then to another.

"These scrolls …… were from the Libraries of Alexandria,

not long after the fall of the Egyptian Kingdom. You will find your Star Travel knowledge here," he said, picking one out. "Here, take a look. They are in hieroglyphics, but you will understand it once you have cleared your mind. Just read the thoughts behind the scribe, just read their thoughts Si Jan, and all will fall into place."

I realised then that Munshi was not just a moth-eaten scribe or librarian as I had first thought. He was another Master. I suppose they were all Masters of one kind or another and so was everyone and everything on this God-made Earth. If only we see the treasures hidden within each other and learn what knowledge every living thing has to offer, Mankind will see a brighter Age.

Jolted back from my short reverie, I returned my gaze to the old papyrus scroll; I looked at the rows and rows of hieroglyphic script with figures of fish, zig zags, falcons and a hippo, numerous seals of office, dots and dashes and whatever else made up the scroll.

"Clear your mind, make it blank, then look again at the scroll, make it blank too," the Munshi advised. I did as he asked.

"Now what are you left with?" he asked.

"Nothing."

"Good! Now all you will see before you is the Mind of the scribe. Now read that!" he ordered.

With my mind making the scroll a blank, the Egyptian scribe's mind was there laid out for me to read, and as my eyes ran along the length of the papyrus, all his thoughts from some five thousand years ago entered me. I was amazed to know what their Civilisation knew so long ago: knowledge about Other Worlds, other Civilisations and other Planets.

If only I knew before how easy it is, no book however foreign would be a task for me to decipher. No wonder he is the Munshi, the scribe, the translator!

We were, and still are, too primitive and arrogant to accept anything higher than ourselves; so instead of learning, we destroyed the very keys to a Paradise already here and waiting. Now, we could only grope in the Darkness of our ignorance, with the hope of building a paradise of our own. The Munshi looked at me and smiled.

"Now do you know how they reached us?"

"Yes, Munshi, I know now. There is no uniform darkness in space. They travelled by sliding along the sheets of darkness, pulled along the planes, riding on the potentials with no effort at all...."

"Enough, Si Jan, enough said. As long as you know and you are satisfied. Man is not yet ready to travel the stars, let it be hidden for a while longer." Then he said, with a finger to his lips: "be quiet, tell nobody!"

"Are you happy now?" the Munshi asked, while looking around the hall. "Here, you will need these two." Taking out two very tattered parchments, he continued: "They are Japanese, and were originally on paper but were transferred onto skin by the Mongolians. They had captured these from their enemies, the Japanese, but their ship sank before they could bring them back to Kublai Khan in China."

"What are they about, Munshi?"

"About how to bring on storms! Like the two big ones that destroyed the Mongolian warships on each occasion when they were out to conquer Japan."

"You mean those two storms the Japanese call their Kamikaze or their Divine Winds?"

"You should know, you were their Captain Ichiro Sato, weren't you ?......... in their last war?"

"How did you know, Munshi?" I asked.

He looked around at the millions of books and scrolls and whatnots in the hall.

"With all these," he said pointing around him, "we know everything."

Chapter Thirteen

"You will now need to learn how to freeze and move Time. I know Pak Samad showed these feats to you sometime ago," the Munshi said as he moved to lift up a thick volume, its cover bound by the skin of a black bear.

"Wow! *Buku Bulu!*" I exclaimed. A fur-wrapped book, as mentioned in stories of Magic and Mystery handed down by the Elders. Such books were rumoured to contain secret Knowledge only accessible to a chosen few.

The Munshi laughed at my impatience and laughed louder at my confusion as I opened the book with trembling hands for all the pages were blank …empty!

"Ha, ha, a book like this is not easy for a thief to read, Si Jan, not that I saying you are one. No, you will only be able to read whatever page we allow you to read, and only in our presence. This is how real secrets are kept."

With that, he flipped open a few pages of the blank book and stopped somewhere in its middle.

"Here read this," he said, pushing the open book back to me. "Read!" he commanded.

I could see nothing but a blank page, yellowed with age.

"Read? What am I to read?"

"This!"

As the Munshi's finger ran along the page, lines of old Jawi script started to surface. Written much like a simplified form of Arabic, the sentences started from the right and kept appearing as Munshi's finger traced on.

It spoke of Time as a malleable Dimension, no more than a play of Darkness and Light, stretchable and yet compressible. It spoke of how to stop its flow for a brief instant or for years, with the power of certain words that control its passage or flow.

The blank pages kept filling up with script as Munshi's finger traced on. I was immersed in these sacred passages and was totally oblivious to time itself. I memorised the sacred words knowing that, sometime in the future, my life might depend on it.

Munshi's finger stopped and the rest of the Book remained blank. "That is all for now," he announced, gently replacing the volume back to its shelf.

"Are the rest of these books also blank?"

"Yes and no. It depends on who needs to read them and, most

importantly, why."

"Why are they always wrapped in bear skin, Munshi?"

"Some are wrapped in goat skins; the really precious ones in bear and three in tiger skins."

"Tiger skins? Where are they?"

The Munshi laughed out loud, showing his aging teeth and receeding gums. "You have to be really special to see them, they are kept in the Queen's bedchamber," slapping me on the back. He appeared happy for a change, his feathery eye brows lifted exposing a pair of ancient but lively eyes. It must have been aeons since someone asked him about those books and aeons since he last mentioned the Queen's bedchamber.

"What is in those three Books, Munshi?"

"Nothing much. The first Book tells how to end this present world; the second tells how to start the next one, and the last Book tells how to return to the Stars."

"And that's nothing much?" I asked incredulously, "nothing much? Those are things that concern the whole world! What if an evil person got hold of the first one, the first book you described, I mean. Who could stop him?"

"Well, Si Jan, we have you, haven't we? You can now stop Time, freeze Time, and speed it up if you wish, so what's the matter? You have the power to prolong the time before the World turns bad enough for an evil one to end it."

"But so can all of you!" I exclaimed, "the lot of you!"

"Yes. And isn't that what this game is all about?"

"All this is just a game?"

"Yes, the Evil ones have as much knowledge as we do. At stake in the game is whether they can prolong the world in a suffering of their making."

"You mean the Evil One's making?" I interrupted.

"Yes, their making. We are striving to keep the world in proper balance and however long in our making," he stressed.

"So, we are the Good people?"

"Yes, that's what we think of ourselves. They think the opposite of us though."

"So, who is right?" I asked, getting slightly confused.

"It depends which way the world leans. It all depends which side the world prefers to lean to. Too much Evil will make us the Bad Ones," he laughed. "Never mind," he continued, "Si Jan, you and your friends can stretch Time to allow this Game to play on until the time comes when the First Book is opened."

"You mean, when we lose?"

"No, when we win."

"Si Jan! Jepun! Time to leave!" Aweh's voice came echoing through the corridors.

"Shall I go?" I asked Munshi. All this about the Game, the Evil Ones and the Three Books in the Queen's Chamber were making me feel uncomfortable. The sight of these millions of books of Learning that ran on for a mile was giving me a headache—the thought of having to read all of them one day.

The Munshi, who must have read my mind patted me on the shoulder: "No, Si Jan, only one more book for you to read; you can come back here when the time comes."

"How do I get here the next time?"

"Sink another boat and wait for another turtle," he joked.

Aweh was at the entrance, laughing when he heard what the Munshi said.

"I hope he behaved, Munshi?"

"He did, and was a good student. He is a credit to you. The protocol was observed at all times."

"Protocol? *Nasbah?*" What is so important about these rules of nasbah? I asked the two of them.

"Si Jan, when that is broken, and each time it is broken........" Aweh was trying hard to explain.

"The Sea will inundate the land. You Japanese call that a *Tsunami*. You understand? *Wakarimasu ka?*" Munshi interrupted.

"Or the land slides into the sea, or man-made soil erosion, Jepun!" added Aweh looking at me seriously, "that happens every time man bites off more than he can chew; but it appears you behaved well and did not ask for more of anything while you were here —be it fish, seaweed, knowledge, or women!"

Munshi glared, half-seriously, at Aweh and they both broke out laughing. I made a mental note, never to eat too much fish, or seaweed, never to build a house by the shore, and never to sleep with any woman from the sea.

The two men looked at my thoughts. "That's a virgin talking!" Aweh announced before the two roared off in laughter again.

I hoped they would both drop dead there and then.

All men over five hundred years old are rogues, I concluded.

Chapter Fourteen

"With the Munshi leading, we moved through the various chambers of freshly gathered seaweed. "Here, this is where you can ascend to the surface. Then latch on to a Grey Wind and go back to Pak Samad."

The turtles were already there, ready and waiting. A warrior came with a tray of beaten silver covered with a cloth of red and black designs. On it lay Aweh's precious pebble. No more a monolith, now just a smooth stone one that you would ignore on any beach.

The Munshi handed it back to Aweh. "Here, your rock! Next time, make it even bigger." Looking sideways at me, he said, with a wink, "we need a few more islands."

"Aweh, when you have time, teach your student more—he clearly has a thirst to learn. He will be a worthwhile pupil, a true warrior in time to come."

Then, patting me on my shoulder, he said: "Si Jan, when you finally go and do battle in the West, show them what real magic is all about."

We grasped his hand and thanked him as the waters rose up in a column carrying us to the surface. The Munshi gave us another wave, and then walked away from view. The sea now covered everything below.

We surfaced in broad daylight, a blue sky above with the tropical sun beating down on the waves and us. The warmth of the air and the lazy flop-flop of the turtles' flippers made us feel rested and ready for sleep. If only we could continue to live like so.

"We can, Si Jan," Aweh said, "when you have completed your tasks and reached the end of your days."

"When will the end of my days come?"

"Ah, only when this world is ready to let you go."

"Can you see into the future, Aweh?" I asked, as this thought just came by.

"Of course, everyone can, but whether the future you see is real or just your own wishful thinking, and whether you are able and strong enough to make the future you wish for come true, that's another story."

I took awhile to mull over what he had said. By then, the turtles arrived at a small outcrop of rocks and sand and a few palm trees. "That's an island," Aweh said. "Anything over the water, one whole year and with at least one tree growing on it, that's an island," he proclaimed.

We forgot about seeing into the future as we alighted from the backs of these two giant turtles, patted their backs, and said our thanks and goodbyes as they turned round in the shallows, gave us a parting glance and silently swam back to the deep.

"Here," said Aweh, picking up a green coconut, "have a drink, there are more on the tree."

We had not used our weapons for a good while. " Kyai Aweng! Parang!" I commanded, and the keris turned into a machete.

"Aweh, why were our weapons useless when we were trapped under that 'Hair Net'?"

"Well, the Evil Ones have their magic and we have ours. We could have devised other ways of escape, but sometimes it is fun to see how far the Evil Ones plan to go and what powers they have. It's all a Game, remember?"

With all the talk about a 'Game' being played by the Good and the Evil, I began to feel the futility of it all. What was I doing with a bunch of near mad mystics if it was all a 'Game' to them?

"War Games! Si Jan. Life is a Game, everything is an illusion, Si Jan. It depends on which part of the illusion, which part of the Book, and which chapter of it that makes you think it real, or not real and just an illusion."

"So,what are you Aweh? Are you real or an illusion?"

"For now, I am real. You are real. Have a drink," he gestured towards my green coconut

The cool juice of the fruit was invigorating. "What about you? Why are you not drinking?"

"Who wants to drink an illusion?" he laughed.

"But this coconut is real, the juice is real!" I protested shaking at the nut for him to see.

"Ah, Si Jan! But I am not!" and like him, his voice simply faded away.

I wasn't sure if I should laugh or cry. Stranded on an island in the middle of nowhere, and my friend was only an illusion? Was the keris, Kyai Aweng, that he made for me an illusion? Was this island an illusion? And worse still, was I just an illusion?

Suddenly a wave of sheer loneliness came over me, but it was followed by a wave of silence and peace that I had never known before.

I felt myself floating in a dark, dark void, amongst stars. I felt totally alone and at peace with a Creation that I had just become able to fathom. I was like a speck of dust, floating silently in a darkened room by myself and in no need for company or help.

I tried to stay in this void for as long as I could, savouring a peace which few mortals ever get to sample. I must have tasted a sample of Immortality, maybe even a sample of God, however short.

"Oi, wake up!" Aweh's voice came barging in on my being, shattering my quiet repose. "Coconut juice and the sun makes one drowsy!"

"I thought you had disappeared, you became an illusion!"

He gave me a smack on the head. "If everything is an illusion, *apa ini*?—what's this?"

"But it was *you* who told me about everything being an illusion. It was *you* who suddenly disappeared from view and now you say that you are *real*?"

"Ah, Si Jan, we have turned the page now, haven't we ? It will be real for a while more."

Gawd! Blast you! Aweh. May you be cursed Aweh! I was at the point of crying, feeling helpless and alone.

"Eh, Si Jan, where would you be without me?" Aweh laughed, as he read my thoughts.

"At least, I would be one happy illusion!" I replied.

It was too late to hear his reply as a Grey Wind tore down on us, whirling us away and taking us towards the Golden Chersonese of the Ancient Greeks, our homeland.

Chapter Fifteen

"The Megalith was afloat when we reached Gunong Ledang. Smoke or mists from the jungle were flowing towards its base and under it when we rounded the corner.

"It was squat on the ground the last time I came," I said.

"Of course, they were away, so the whole place was closed. Now that they are home, the rock floats to announce that they are in business! Your dear wife awaits!"

The mere mention of Sri brought on a series of mixed reactions, of expectation and then of apprehension. Was she really my wife in the real sense or was she just another illusion? Aweh gave me a nudge and a wink: "Both, she is both," as we entered their midst.

The place looked organised for a conflict. There were no hints of a previous celebration, no trace of even a faded blossom on the floor. Men were dressed as warriors, carrying their long narrow shields that were covered with hardened shagreen or sharkskin. They were all armed with mandaus, those deadly swords of the Borneo head-hunters, the Ibans. Each hilt had festoons of hair from scalps of their last victims.

This is business! So who are they out to do battle with?

"Ah! Aweh! Si Jan! You're back!" Pak Samad`s voice boomed. "Just in time! We were worried that the two of you would not make it. Especially you, Si Jan!"

"Me?"

"Yes. They have captured Sri, and now we plan to rescue her. You'd better get ready! Aweh, did you bring the stone?" Aweh nodded in affirmation.

"How did it happen?" I asked.

"Well, Sri was out gathering flowers from the peaks of Tampin for the coming festival, when one of them, the Dark Ones, transformed himself into one of our ladies, while another transformed himself into a tiger. Sri went after the beast to save her 'friend' and that got her deeper and deeper into their midst. She has been missing these last four days."

"You see, emotions can drain one's power. Sri was so concerned about the welfare of her friend that she became careless and became trapped. The Evil Ones prey on one's weaknesses, so be careful. That is why I ask you to practice detachment," Aweh cautioned.

"Don't worry, Si Jan. We will get her back. We haven't had a battle for a long time. This should be good! Si Jan, go and prepare yourself!" he commanded.

The war drums started and men formed into battle lines. I was given the battle colours to wear, a charmed shirt of black and yellow stripes and the usual black pants.

"Aweh! You will lead the second column! Si Jan, you take the third, the rest come under me! Pak Samad ordered.

"Ready?" he shouted. Our silence meant that we were.

"*Um hun askarang betang kati angni sang lebah!*" he intoned, while the war drums went on beating.

There was a buzzing sound and some general commotion amongst us. I could feel my being transform as I started to shrink and change shape. Something was vibrating behind my back.... I no longer had hands! I had become ..... no one would ever believe me .... I had become a bee!

Now transformed into an angry swarm of these stinging insects, we hovered for awhile over our campsite, and led by Pak Samad`s column, flew out from the Rock. Aweh led the next and I just followed Aweh's as we charged out into the darker regions of the jungle.

We flew through jungle thickets and streams, over clumps of bamboo and fruit trees, guided by thoughts that must have come from Pak Samad, our leader. We swung from one side of mountain to the next, heading North for Tampin. Looking about me, we were one formidable swarm, fuelled by anger and the expectation of a coming slaughter.

What would our enemies be like? What would they have transformed into? I prayed that they would have no knowledge of an insect spray! If they had, what would become of us? Of me? I wasn't too keen to die as a bee in the Malayan jungle, to be food for the ants.

How could a bee make love to Sri? Without stinging her?

With my mind full of these useless thoughts, I lead my column on. Somewhere, in the back of my mind, I could hear the combined laughter of Pak Samad and Aweh.

May the two of you crash into a rock or a tree!

"Get ready! Jepun! They are just ahead!" came Pak Samad's thought in reply. "Get ready!"

Chapter Sixteen

Our swarm flew over a limestone crop and down towards what looked like a sugar cane plantation that stretched for miles. As we hovered, the leading column with Pak Samad in charge made its descent. We followed suit and, just as we were about ten feet from the ground, Pak Samad let out a roar "Songsang!"

We dropped to the ground, or rather tumbled down, not as bees but as warriors, fully-armed and ready.

Pak Samad dressed as a Chieftain led the charge into the thick sugar cane growth.

It did not take long for the battle to begin as equally fearsome cries came to meet us.

A face, painted black with a white stripe across its middle, rose up from the foliage to meet me. The man carried a spear and a shield, much wider than our warriors' shields. He screamed as he stabbed at me, and screamed again when he realised his efforts were useless against an Orang Kebal, an invulnerable being.

By then, Kyai Aweng had been transformed into my Kanemoto. I could see the whites of his horrified eyes as he tried to step back into the bush. Alas, he was too late as my sword cut him down.

After the first kill, it was just a repetition of the same effort or procedure for me. Hunt them down, allow them to make the first move, and I the second and, always, the final one.

All our men did the same, though the foliage was much too thick to observe their action, but I could sense a general retreat of the Evil Ones towards the mouth of the limestone cave.

Over the din of battle, Aweh's voice rang clear: "We follow!" Like a wave, the sugar cane stalks were bent down as we charged at the retreating foe.

They made for the cave as our warriors charged on; the sugar cane field thinned the nearer we got to its mouth, and we could see more of them hurrying in.

"Not bad, eh, Si Jan?" Aweh said when I caught up with him. "Not bad, eh? We can fight when provoked—now to find Sri!" Pointing with his keris to the cave's opening, he said that she must be inside.

Not many of the fleeing enemy troops made it into the mouth

of the cave, as our warriors caught up with them from behind.

Amidst the screams of the fallen and the victors alike, most were cut down by our mandaus.

"The best time to fight is the daytime, when the Evil Ones' powers are weak. Never take them on at night," panted Pak Samad, as he came up from behind. I could see that he had over exerted himself somewhat: "Si Jan, go and find Sri while we take a rest here."

I nodded my willingness and moved on. The canes were getting sparse as I neared the limestone outcrop so the going was easier.

The cave, now littered with the wounded and dying foe, was dark and dank. It smelt badly of bat droppings or guano. I could still hear the sounds of battle in the deeper recesses, of sword against sword or spear. Every so often, I could hear the thud of a shield used in defence, and a scream or cry of victory when a head was taken. *Gory stuff, these tribal conflicts.*

One of our men, Suling, gave a shout "Si Jan! She is here!" There could be only one lady in this whole exercise. Suling used his blood-soaked mandau to point at a hole in the ground, where Sri was buried up to her neck, her eyes and nose plugged with mud. Only her mouth was open to breathe and had we not rescued her at that time, she would have been dead within an hour. Used to a land of the proverbial milk and honey, being entombed in a dark, dank guano-filled cave would do any Fairy in.

"Quick! Suling, call for more men and help me get her out!" I yelled.

It did not take us long to free her. She was barely breathing when I carried her out of the cave. By then, Pak Samad and Aweh had arrived on the scene, and concluded that I must take her back as soon as I could. Pak Samad, now recovered, stood on a small mound and summoned the fastest Grey Wind that he could find. It came faster than one would find a taxi in any big city. He had the Power and he made the call. Simple.

"Be quick!" he said as he helped us up. I carried Sri close to my chest in one arm and with the other hand clung on to the Wind.

"Kembali!" Pak Samad shouted to the Wind as we took off, heading for our Gunong Ledang, leaving everything and everyone behind.

Just then, a dark cloud issued from the depths of the cave. Flying foxes! Large bats with wingspans up to two metres with bodies to match and they were heading our way. Pak Samad and Aweh found another Grey Wind and came alongside us, this time bringing Suling. He had never ridden the Grey Wind so he greeted me again, but with his eyes closed.

As the cloud of giant bats neared, I could make out their features. They were not bats, but the same evil men we had been fighting on the ground just a few minutes earlier. Armed with spears and showing their fangs, they flew alongside us. Much like a bat's wings, theirs was a skin that stretched from their arms to their feet.

I passed Sri to Suling: "Here, hold on to Sri and the Wind, for your life depends on it!" I ordered.

Now with one arm free, I was able to join Pak Samad and Aweh in confronting those beings. The first group ignored the three of us and headed straight for Suling and Sri.

I managed to slash at them when they got near. They fell screaming as the next wave came towards Aweh and Samad. The three of us, now riding on the same Wind fought them as they came, hacking at whatever that presented itself. I soon realised that their weak point was the membrane that made up their wing. A slight cut or tear would make them helpless, and they would just fall to the ground. With their wings torn, they were useless for further flight or fight.

Once we had all identified their weak point, it did not take us too long to defeat our attackers. A small cut in their wing and they fell off like "lice from a buffalo," to quote Aweh.

"Let the others go!" Pak Samad ordered as the remainder flew away. "We'll need them to fight another day."

I suppose he was right—what use is a warrior without wars to fight?

"All should be safe and well from here on," he laughed. "I must leave you to bring back our troops........as bees!"

Gunong Ledang our Fairy Mountain came into view, and we wasted no time hurrying back to the Rock. This time, the women folk were all at the entrance, anxious for a glimpse of Sri.

"She is still alive!" announced Aweh as we lowered Sri onto a waiting mat. "Quick, fetch us water and the *Daun Balek Sedar*—the herb that revives."

Sri's face was first washed with water, and the bunch of magic leaves brushed her still beautiful features. Her eyes opened for the first time after so many days of being caked in mud. She looked around and recognised the Princess, then her eyes met mine. She tried to smile, but weakness and exhaustion overtook her and she lapsed once again into unconsciousness.

A nectar of some kind was dribbled into her still opened mouth and then some water from the Spring. A healthier change came on her before long. Her breathing became more noticeable before sunset, and she was taken to the bath enclosure by the ladies in attendance.

The dark swarm of bees returned and were soon transformed back to our warriors. None were lost in that battle so there was much back-slapping amongst the men. Though many had their baju or shirts shredded and torn, only a few suffered scratches that needed attention.

Pak Samad came up to us with his old box of Rokok Puchok. "Time for a smoke, Si Jan. *Ayoh! Ayoh!*" He called on the others to come.

We were a few hundred, and seated around in this large circle of warriors, I was as proud as a peacock to be amongst the men. I knew I had become a warrior, much like them, if not as good.

"They are good warriors, but bad travellers, Si Jan," Pak Samad interrupted my thoughts. "So bad so that we had to turn ourselves and them into bees. There is no way that we could have taken them on our Grey Winds."

"They would fall off like lice from a buffalo," interjected Aweh.

There was a hearty round of laughter and a few of the men went buzzing into each other's ears.

With a little Fairy Magic, there was enough Puchok and tobacco in that little box for us all, and we sat around smoking and helping ourselves with the drinks and food till the jungle cock crowed in the dawn.

Chapter Seventeen

It must have been two days before Sri recovered and felt well enough to meet me. It was the longest two days of my life, waiting to get a glimpse of her through the curtains of the Princess's Court where no men were allowed in.

My mind was elsewhere during the cock fights that the men put up for entertainment, even when the bird given to me made little of his rivals. I let others do the cheering every time it won. My heart was elsewhere.

"Si Jan, thank you for rescuing me, Si Jan," were her first words when she emerged from the Princess's chamber.

She fell into my arms and hugged me hard.

The usual company were kind enough to fade away, leaving us alone as we walked to our old hut down the track. Holding hands, we said little until we entered our simple dwelling that was constructed for us by Aweh when we were married.

She turned towards me and with tear-brimmed eyes, gave me a long lingering kiss that seemed to speak volumes.

Our beings merged. The Space that separated us in the Universe became an uniform one. Peace descended and we stayed forever locked in a corner of Infinity.

Now, tearing ourselves apart and gasping for air, we looked at each other and managed an embarrassed laugh.

"That was good, wasn't it?" I asked. She nodded a yes, and we kissed again.

Slowly, she pulled me on to our bed, let down her hair and helped me undress. I was nervous and clumsy—all hands and all feet.

"This is it!" I said to myself, as she smilingly undid her blouse and sarong, and still looking at me, pulled me down on her.

She was patient as she taught me the ways of making a woman happy, very happy, and I was a quick learner.

We must have spent an aeon on the bed, bathed in a mellowness of two rested souls. Time may have called, looked kindly on us, the two lovers, left us alone and moved on.

"Thirsty?" she asked. "Just a bit" I replied. Now clad in her flimsy underwear, she crawled to the edge of the bed for the pitcher and clay cup. "Here, from our sacred Spring. Drink deep."

With just a few sips of the cool fluid, I became aroused again.

She laughed and made a dive for me, once more.

I have no idea how many times that I drank from that wonderful cup, not that anyone was counting.

It was almost dark when we decided it best that we stop, even for a while, light up the oil lamp in the hut and go meet the others up the slope.

"Just one more sip?" I protested. Sri laughed as she was almost fully dressed by then. "Si Jan, that stream flows for eleven months of the year, how much water can you drink?"

We emerged from our hut, like two young lovers, holding hands as we walked up the slope towards the clearing.

"Eh, Sri, the next time Aweh teases me about being a virgin, I'm going to kill him!"

She laughed as she clung closer to my side.

"I think the whole world knows by now that you are one of their best."

Chapter Eighteen

We were just in time for the victory celebrations. The whole place was festooned with flowers gathered from the jungle. Pak Samad and the Fairy Princess were seated on a raised dais, and both smiled knowingly at us when we entered the clearing.

Aweh came over and patted me on the back. "Happy now, Si Jan?" Sri gave my arm a squeeze and left to attend to the Princess. I took a seat amongst a group of men and joined them in smoking our reed cigarettes.

The giant gong sounded and the drums beat a slow rhythm as a line of fully dressed warriors came into view. We were then witness to a well-choreographed display of martial discipline. The men moved in unison as though in a trance, wielding their mandaus and brandishing their shields in complete concentration, oblivious of the admiring crowd.

They were there to perform for the Princess and no one else. Their movements spoke of the battle just passed; they wielded their swords in slow motion and raised their shields at certain times to defend themselves from the now imaginary blows that were rained on them by our enemy.

One by one, as though on cue, the men exited from the centre of the clearing when the Gong sounded the end. The gamelans then started, as two lines of beautiful girls aged from ten to perhaps twenty appeared. Dressed in their finest silks, they moved in time to the changes of the gamelan's tempo, gyrating and twirling, much like the falling blossoms from a Flame of the Forest tree on its way to the ground. With their colourful garments to match, it was a magical sight to behold.

The music continued even after the dancers left.

Plates of porcelain and celadon, piled high with food were brought out for the feast that was to follow. I could see that the utensils were from the Chinese Ming and Yuan periods, their vivid cobalt blues and the crackling glaze on the celadon betraying their origin.

"Each plate on the ground costs thousands of dollars," I whispered to the man beside me.

"Thousands?" he asked with a laugh.

"Who wants thousands or millions? The more money you make, the more enemies you have," he added, tucking into a piece of coconut cake. "This is better," pointing to the bite he had just taken.

"If you want money, ask Aweh, he makes money for a laugh," he advised.

"Yes, I have seen him do it," I replied, "and Pak Samad too."

"Only for a reason, Si Jan, only for a reason."

"Can you make money from nothing, like them?"

"I have no reason to," was his answer.

It was later in the night when Aweh came to sit beside me that I broached the subject again: "Eh, Aweh, can you teach me how to make money?"

He almost fell back on his haunches in horror." What! You Si Jan? You want to make money to be rich?"

I could sense his total disappointment in me. *What a failure, what a waste of effort in bringing this young pup all this way and all he wants is to be rich and make money? Where did we go wrong when we took him as one of our own?*

I read his thoughts.

"No Aweh, I don't mean to make money to be rich. I just want to know how it is done by you and Pak Samad." The relief on his face was discernible.

"Here, what's this?" he asked as he picked up a stone.

"A stone," I replied.

"Just a stone?"

"Yes, just a stone."

"What kind of stone?"

"An ordinary stone," I said,"a small piece of rock, just a stone."

"Yes, you are right. To you, it's just a stone. A small piece of rock, did you say? But to me, it is just a small piece of gold, look hard at it, Si Jan!" he ordered.

I did. It was still a piece of rock, pale and spotted with darker areas of brown.

"Look harder!" he ordered, still staring at the piece of stone.

I followed, gazing at it on the palm of his hand with all the concentration I could muster, willing it to be gold.

"Now relax your gaze, stupid," he whispered.

I did so and there on his hand was a smooth piece of gold, a sizeable nugget.

"It only happened when your determination to want to see a rock had waned, allowing your Mind to create a form that your Will desired. Now do you understand, Jepun?" he scolded.

How my world, my sense of Reality, changed that night. How my belief in all that was an illusion increased from then on.

Two days later, Pak Samad came by as Sri and I were at the door of our little hut peeling petai nuts for our first attempt at a home-cooked meal.

"Why do you need to cook, Sri? One of the ladies will do it for you," he said. "Go up the slope and just tell them what Si Jan and you desire and it will be done"

"It's just something we thought of doing together."

"Ah, I forgot—still love birds, you two?" he laughed.

"I heard that Aweh has taught you how to make gold out of a rock?"

"Yes, will you show me how you make dollar notes from the leaves of a tree?"

"Not any tree, Si Jan, only some," and pointing to a branch of wild cinnamon, he continued, "that one would be ideal. Come along and let me show you. Let Sri do the women's work," he teased. "Always choose the right colour leaf for the right kind of paper money you need. Red or pink for one value and green for the other. Only do so when there is a real need, like the last time when we had to board the train in Tapah Road for you to save those wretched lives. The magic will only work when it knows that your need is genuine, genuine for the benefit of the Universe, Si Jan, and not for you or your ego. Do you understand, Jepun?"

He collected a small bunch of the young pink leaves and gave them to me.

"Put them in your pocket; now think of them as ten dollar notes only, all the time. So when the need comes, take them out and they will be what you want them to be."

I did as he ordered. With the soft leaves in my trouser pocket, I found it impossible to think them as anything other than cool, young leaves from that wild cinnamon tree.

"Now, Jepun! Walk away from me, walk up to that clump of bamboo. Then turn around and walk back and just look at me, without thinking about those ten dollar notes in your pocket; just think of me and of Sri."

I walked on as ordered, dragging my feet in my uncertainty. I reached the clump of bamboo and turned back.

Pak Samad was gone; only Sri stood there, her arms wishing me back.

"What happened? Where is Pak Samad?" I yelled. She just waved her arms about: "Somewhere!"

"Now, where are those ten dollar notes?" she asked when I reached her. I fumbled for the bunch of paper in my pocket.

"Are you sure you didn't drop any?" she asked with some concern.

"No, they are all here, all ninety dollars," said I, counting them in my hand. Sri laughed out loud.

Chapter Nineteen

"I suppose he needs just one more lesson here before we send him home," Aweh told Pak Samad.

"Yes, no point in him trying to fly with only one wing."

I was quite at a loss as to what they were talking about.

"Well, soon Jepun, you will have to join, or rather rejoin, the world of mortals, the world of Man. You will have to live a normal-looking life although you are one of us. There are things you will need to do in their presence to regain the Balance that they have lost, and as such, you will need a profession to be able to make a living amongst them and to be 'normal' in their eyes. You can't go around making gold from pebbles, and cash from leaves in the world of Man."

"Soon," Pak Samad announced, "you will be taken to meet Badang, our Medicine Man. It's best that you learn how to really heal before you are taught their Western ways of healing."

It suddenly became clear what these two old warriors were on about. All these wars, undersea adventures, and being with Sri had made me forget that I had a life waiting outside the Fairy Realm. And furthermore, I had a task to fulfil in that world before I could return to it and be one of them.... eventually.

Sri smiled at my predicament. "Go on, Si Jan, fulfil your tasks, I will be beside you and we can come back when we are ready."

The mere mention of 'we' was assuring to me.

"Right! When are we meeting this Badang?"

"Tomorrow,"Aweh said.

When we were left alone, I asked Sri exactly what and who Badang healed, since the Fairy Folk could live forever.

"He heals the sickness in everything," came her short answer. I left it at that and we spent a pleasant night, with Sri teaching me some jungle songs.

"Badang lives alone, and one can only get to see him if he allows it," Aweh said while leading us up a steep slope, through a thicket of bamboo and palm, before descending down to a rock-strewn ravine beside a raging river.

"Datok! *Badang! Kita di sini!*—we are here!" Aweh shouted across the thundering roar. "Badang!"

As though someone had turned off a tap, the river suddenly slowed its flow and the water was only at our ankles

“Come on! Let’s cross!” Aweh hurried us on. Sri had her hand on my shoulder for support and, giggling like a schoolgirl, tried stepping on the tops of some exposed rocks.

She had told me in the night that being allowed to follow me wherever I went was something new for her. Confined all these years to just serving the Princess on Gunong Ledang, the Fairy Mountain, she knew little of the world outside their realm.

So, this little trek with men, and not with other ladies-in-waiting, was an adventure to her. “No more danger of being captured again because I’ll be with you, Si Jan,” she had whispered. I didn’t dare tell her that I was only a so-so warrior as I went for another sip of water from her magic pitcher and snuffed down the oil lamp.

As in all traditions and cultures of old, healers, medicine men or priests live away from their tribe. The reasoning is that they should be sheltered from day-to-day distractions of community life. Left on their own, they can be pure in their art or craft and maintain their power. Their community supports them, making sure they want for nothing, living a frugal existence in a life so chosen. In return, they help their community in spiritual affairs.

Those were the unspoken rules for any mystic or medicine man. Their powers depend on their keeping these rules of behaviour; if they break them, they become no more than charlatans banished by their tribe or community to eke out a living by deception in the world of Men.

Badang emerged from his hut. He was a stout man, ageless, though his flowing white hair and his pale, greenish-tinged skin told of years lived in the wilderness.

He recognised Aweh and made a slight bow to Sri before settling his eyes on me.

"Ah, Si Jan, we meet finally."

Before I could say anything, he added: "I healed your Mother when she was heavy with you. The Evil Ones tried to prevent you from being born, Si Jan."

It came as a shock, to hear him say that. Evil Ones? Trying to snuff out my life.......before I could be reborn? I felt a sudden surge of anger rising from the depths of my being, not that I knew who those 'Evil Ones' were or even looked like. Surely they were not the types we had slaughtered in that limestone cave? It would be an insult to have those as my enemies.

First my anger, then my hatred, rose up from deeper parts of my being. Somehow I felt these emotions erupting from my past lives. Captain Ichiro Sato's fury rose to the surface as I struggled to retain my composure; then there was the anger from lifetimes of other beings I never knew I was before.

The overwhelming protest in my soul was that of the audacity of these Evil Ones in trying to stop my continued existence in this World of Man.

I managed to calm myself as Sri held me and Aweh patted my back. "*Sabar, Si Jan, sabar, menahan, Si Jan*—be patient and endure."

Badang smiled and said nothing. He reached out his hand in the air and, as Aweh did earlier, brought down bunches of bananas, rambutans and even a bunch of mata kuchings.

"I know you love your longans, especially the dried ones your Fat Aunt buys you, everytime she wins the lottery. But longans come from China, Si Jan, I hope these smaller mata kuchings will do." Aweh laughed at my surprised look.

"So, you knew or know of my Fat Aunt?"

"Of course, we were all around your bedside when you were born. Your mother was at death's door even then." I felt such hurt on hearing that my birth had caused her so much pain and ill-health. I was not too keen on Badang's fruits, a few of which I ate in silence out of courtesy as I sat to hear more from him.

"Despite your past life, you were not too healthy as a child, rather sickly in fact. The Evil Ones followed every step you made, and so did we, just to keep you from straying into their path and letting them win.

"Yes, they even enlisted those friends of yours to distract you, to corrupt you when you were a teen. It was good that they failed and you are what you are today. Had you fallen, all your past would have been lost. All the powers you had before would not surface and no new learning would be possible in this lifetime."

Aweh changed the subject, sensing that I was getting weighed down by these revelations.

"Sri, will you tidy up the room Badang has made for the two of you? It's in a hut higher up the slope under the Royal palms, that's where the two of you will live while he learns his trade."

"Trade?" I looked at Aweh.

"As a mystic healer—that will be one wing for this lazy bird to fly on!" Aweh shared his joke with Badang.

"When you go back and become the doctor your father wants you to be, that will be your second wing, so you can really fly then."

Aweh stood up and circled us slowly with arms outstretched pretending to be an eagle.

"Maybe he will end up flying like a chicken, who knows?" Badang joked.

Sri had her hand over her mouth, trying hard not to let me see her laugh.

Chapter Twenty

Sri and I came down to Badang's hut early next morning. Aweh had left sometime in the night. He went by way of the Hari Kong as he had other warriors to meet.

Badang was up and preparing our first meal of the day—boiled sweet potatoes and water. "Simple living, high thinking" he said with a smile and motioned us to sit on his tattered mat.

Below us, the jungle was thousand hues of green. We could see a flock of parrots in flight, with their colourful display of red and green, and hear their calls to each other.

The gibbons had already begun their daily chorus; their Malay name of 'Wak-wak' so appropriate to their nature; one can hear them for miles in the jungle as they keep each other abreast of their position amongst the thick foliage, so thick that only sound and not sight is detectable.

Badang pointed to that huge boulder down below. "Si Jan,

look at that rock. Isn't it miserable looking?" he asked.

"I suppose so."

"Why? Why do you agree that it is so?"

"Well, it looks forlorn and out of place, one side is jagged and mud-smeared, while the other is clean," I replied, not knowing what else to say. I just felt it looked miserable, but had no other way to describe why.

"Why don't you do something about it then?" Badang asked.

"Do what with it?"

"Turn it around for a start!"

"How?"

He nearly hit my head with a boiled sweet potato. "Knowledge learnt must not be compartmentalised. It should be used, applied, at all times. Aweh taught you how to do it in Papua, now do it as he taught you."

I suppose that was my first lesson with Badang. I slid down the slope, patted the rock and drew the sacred signs on its face and watched it shrink to the size of a brick. Then turning it around, I moved it into a position where I felt it more comfortable in its surroundings and made it regrow to its original size before returning to Badang and Sri. They both nodded their approval. "Yes, that looks happier," Badang said finally.

"That rock was sick, Jepun, and you have cured it. The same goes for Man, like that rock, fate can throw a person into a place in life not to his liking, but he may be helpless to do anything about it. So he is sick in heart, body and soul. See how a slight twist might change things?

"Curing a man is not about moving him from one place to another, or giving him a new job for his old. It's all about shifting his outlook wherever he may be, and that might make the difference between sickness and health.

"To move a man, who is just like that rock, so full of self and ego, will be a hard thing to do. So first you have to shrink his idea of his self-importance, just as you overcame the boulder's idea of its form by those sacred symbols. No one, nothing, stands alone, and once you have brought him that realisation, he will be as small as the smallest particle in the Universe, so he can be helped."

I was beginning to see the interconnection between each and everything. We and everything can be malleable, if only one knows how. That, I suppose, is where the 'Real' Magic comes in.

"Everything is energy, nothing else that constitutes form. It is the Will and Consciousness of a parcel of that Universal Energy that creates a form; the more the energy, Si Jan, the more the life of a form. It can become not just a rock, but a living thing. Do you understand?"

Sitting there with Badang and Sri, I was beginning to comprehend a bit more of the Mysteries of the Universe and of

Life itself—that nothing was independent and so we were all interlinked. Whether we are 'Good' or 'Bad', we all have a part to play in the general scheme of things.

Nothing dies and everything gets recycled.

I was suddenly quite ashamed of my killing spree in that old church in Northumberland, slaughtering everyone who had charged at me. I was ashamed of how I had taken one life after another, and yet Pak Samad and Sri had allowed me to, knowing that it was just an exercise so that I could learn this lesson later on.

Sri read my thoughts and gave my knee a shake: "If it was a bad thing, we would have stopped you. We just wanted to see how far you would go for us and how soon you would get to learn this lesson from Badang."

"We are all packets of energy, good or bad," she continued. "So, you may call it a 'game' Si Jan, if you wish to. But they, the Evil Ones, were bad, when they sought to overcome the Balance of Good and Evil, making it all theirs, so that is why we needed you to destroy them, some of them."

"What about the last 'war' we fought a few days ago to rescue you?"

She answered without looking at me: "Ah, that was a bad patch of Energy overcoming us in a most unusual way, but we allowed many of our enemies to get away. If not, wouldn't we be just like them, except that we'd be wanting only the Good for the whole world?

"So, I suppose only in some places—like your Fairy Realm—are the fully 'Good' allowed, while only the fully 'Bad' are allowed in other places?"

"Yes, Si Jan, you are getting the idea. It is just that the bad patches are expanding faster than the good ones, and that is where we need you to help."

"Me? Needed?" I thought to myself, feeling a tinge of importance and pride.

"Oi!" Badang cautioned, "that's when you will lose, stay neutral, detached to what anyone says—no anger, no pride, no joy!"

I might as well be a rock, I said to myself.

"Rocks have joys and sorrows too, stupid," Badang said. "Just look at that boulder below."

I did, and could almost see it smile.

"Now, you are getting in tune with the Universe. Try to read *it*, and understand *it* further. That will be your next lesson. *Ayoh!*—come! Let's take a walk through the jungle, it's almost noon and time to gather something from the Pokok Seruling."

The Wak waks had stopped their calling and the jungle awaited our next move.

Chapter Twenty One

"Pokok Seruling?" I asked Sri as we followed Badang along the jungle track. "You will need its help to start being a Healer. Be patient and you will see," she said.

The trek took us up a small hill where the vegetation was sparse and the ground dry.

Badang stopped to take his bearings from a lonely tree at the top. "Take a line from the base of this tree to that rock below, head in that general direction, and listen."

"Listen?"

"With your heart, Badang meant, with your heart," Sri said, patting her own chest.

I stilled my thoughts and, true enough, before long I could hear a small crowd of men busy at work and talking. Their voices got louder and louder as we descended the slope heading for the rock below.

Badang stopped halfway down, looked at us and smiled. Pointing his parang at a gnarled branch of a small tree, he gave us a wink, "*Pokok Seruling*" he whispered, "the Flute Tree."

The voices stopped as we came closer to the branch.

"It is called the Flute Tree because of the numerous holes in its branches that play tunes or whistle when the wind blows through them. Its guardians are always hard at work this time of day, and will rest when the ground cools.

"*Sipatulangi!*" Badang shouted to the branch. I thought him a bit mad and looked back at Sri. She had a finger on her lip

"Shhh. Quiet"

"*Sipatulangi!*" Badang shouted again.

"*Siapa tu?*—who's that?" came a reply as a tiny head appeared from one of the holes.

The head of an ant! A talking ant?

What a shock, but, being with these Mystics and Fairies and all that had happened these last few days, I was quite prepared for anything.

Though small in size, the ant's voice was loud and clear in my mind.

Badang started to introduce us to the Colony as more heads emerged from the holes.

"This man is Si Jan, my new student, and his wife here is Sri, from the Fairy Mountain, a lady-in-waiting to the Princess of Gunong Ledang. Si Jan will need your help to be a healer of men; as such, we have come for the black pearl."

"Does he deserve it?" asked another ant.

"Yes, he has been a good student of Aweh and Pak Samad and has learnt the crafts of a warrior. He knows how to kill and has killed. Now he needs to learn how to heal as he will be leaving us soon to complete his task on this Earth."

I felt that this talk of my "task" was rather unfair without telling me what it was about in the first place. I longed for a chance to ask, but found none.

All the ants disappeared back into the holes and we could hear them arguing and screaming at each other.

A hush descended amongst them, then we could hear the sounds of them busy at work.

The head of one reappeared: "Get ready!" it said, and was gone again.

"Si Jan, put out your hand under the branch. No, cup your two hands! Yes, under that branch and wait," Badang instructed.

I had not suffered such torture before, to stand with arms outstretched in the tropical sun, waiting for God knows what to fall into my hands. It may have been an hour or two, but it felt like twenty years to me. My arms and shoulders ached, right down to the small of my back. Badang and Sri had found shade and sat to watch, as I stood there like a fool on orders from an ant and this Mystic Healer.

I looked towards Badang and Sri for help but they ignored me. After what felt like an eternity, Badang got up and came to me: "*Sabar, Si Jan, sabar*—be patient!" How I hated that word. Sabar!

Badang looked at me and smiled: "If the Universe can wait a billion years for that leaf on that branch to fall, why can't you just wait a while longer?"

My mind boggled at such a thought. I felt so ashamed at my own impatience and self concern. Just who was I in the vastness of the Universe?

I realised then that I would do whatever the Universe asked me to, but first it must show me how.

"Just to live, Si Jan, and help others live too," Badang answered as he walked away; once again, he had heard my thoughts.

The heat of the day had diminished somewhat as the sun began its descent. A cool wind blew up the slope and stirred a little dust devil beside my feet—those little whirlwinds that used to scare us when we were kids were now a welcome distraction.

A small buzz of excitement came on as a thousand ants emerged from the holes and stood on the branch, now black and heavy with their bodies. A voice boomed in my head: "Si Jan! Get ready!"

Something rolled out from one of the holes and fell on to my hand. A black pearl, not more bigger than the size of a green bean!

"Si Jan, swallow it!" Badang shouted as he got up while Sri followed close behind. "Swallow it!"

I did as told. A wave of change came over me when I did. I felt transformed, bright as a star in a world that was now totally different with my new set of vision. Everything had an aura of coloured rainbows. Some trees had rainbows of a darker green aura while some had more yellow. The rocks had a redder aura than the sand at my feet. Badang had an aura of gold, and Sri just a cloud of stars.

I thought that I could hear the ants cheer when I turned to thank them, but they were already busy going back into their tree.

Fat Aunt's teaching came home to me: "When you have done something good, disappear and wait not for thanks or applause…." I supposed it applies to ants as well.

"Now, Si Jan, we can teach you how to heal, but you needed the black pearl from the dwellers of the Pokok Seruling to really see. No point teaching a blind man how to drive, is there?"

Chapter TwentyTwo

Now armed with a new vision of the world, I had to be led by Sri along the track as everything had an aura of one kind or another. I was like a blind man who had suddenly been given sight. The new world that I now saw dazzled me. My steps were childlike, unsure if I should step on anything that had an aura or light.

"You will get used to it, Si Jan, it will all soon fade as the days go by and will only see what and when you want to see." Badang assured me.

"Always have a calm mind, never strain your vision then slowly turn your head sideways as you gaze on your subject and you will see what you want to see—you will see his aura, his past and even his future before you formulate a way of helping him. You have to help everyone who comes to you. Be they the good or bad. For the bad, turn them into good people before you can help them."

"Good people?" I asked.

"Yes, good people are those who are happy to share this world with everyone and everything without reserve and selfishness. They are just happy and content to just live their lives and help others live as well."

"So who are the bad people?" I felt myself like a child with that question, but I wanted to hear Badang's definition.

"Bad people, when we say 'Bad people', we mean those who think this world belongs to them alone, their race, their colour or their flag. They have no time for anyone or anything that is not like them. They have no regard for anyone or anything but themselves. Such people destroy everything without thought or concern, be they other humans, trees, animals or even our Bumi, our Mother Earth."

"Don`t forget, Si Jan, Mother Earth is alive. She will one day be forced to respond."

"Soon, there will be more earthquakes, more floods and other natural disasters. That will be how Mother Earth reacts to the selfishness of such greedy Men," Sri added, her hand still in mine and leading me on.

"Your task and that of Aweh and others who can still kill on both sides of the Mystic curtain will be to stop such wanton destruction of our world. Our job, on this side of the Mystic divide, is to stop the Evil Ones from helping the Bad people succeed on their human plane."

Things were becoming clearer to me. We, the warriors on this side of the Hari Kong, would do our job, while those full blown mystics would battle away on their side.

It sounded fun to me and I couldn't help but smile. I had fought in my last life as Captain Ichiro Sato, and probably had done the same during hundreds of other lifetimes, sometimes with the sword and othertimes with the pen. I could sense that even if I were to have a thousand more lifetimes, each and every day would be a battle for me.

Badang read my thoughts and smiled: " No, Jepun, only one lifetime left. This life, so live well and fight well."

"What comes after that?" I asked.

"You`ll see, my Jepun, you'll see" Badang laughed; Sri pinched my hand and smiled.

Our progress home was slow as I stumbled on most of the way. "Si Jan, look... Kayu Tas*!* Your first friend." Badang stopped at a slim shrub growing on the poorest soil on the slope. It glowed red and emitted an aura of orange and gold.

The stem, only as thick as a broom handle looked dry with withered leaves that felt like sandpaper when I touched it.

"Look at its base and see its guardians, the black scorpions and centipedes. Plants with power always throw a challenge to the gatherer. Only if you are brave and strong, will you succeed in collecting it. Most men would avoid such plants and steer clear without exploring it further. Many would have heard of Kayu Tas, but few would have seen it in its natural state, much less have succeeded in gathering one.

"Now is the right time for collecting it" he continued. "Go on, move them away from the base of the stem and dig it out, right to the very tip of its root."

I knew a scorpion's sting or a bite from a centipede would send me back through the back doors of their Hari Kong and away into Oblivion.

"Go on, Si Jan, we need to be back before it gets dark and we are getting hungry. Sri has to cook dinner."

I made a grab for the first bunch of centipedes and scorpions and threw them as far as I could from the shrub, giving them no time to respond. The remaining made a dash for me but I stayed calm and gathered them one by one and as fast as I could threw them away in every direction.

I could see them making their way back to the base of the stem. With my parang, I dug as fast as I could, knowing that my life really hung on my efforts.

I managed to reach the end of its tap root before the first centipede reached me and, with a cry of victory, lifted the plant out for Badang to see. Sri clapped and jumped for joy. Those infernal insects stopped their advance and moved into the undergrowth.

"Kayu Tas! Now pray tell what am I to do with it?" I said looking at Badang.

"Use it to diagnose an ailment, use it to banish a spirit, to expose a 'were tiger', or just to scratch your back," came his answer.

I could sense that we were all getting weary after this long day in the heat and this place was no place for any more lessons.

I followed them along the track home using the Kayu Tas as my walking stick. Somehow, my steps became more firm, my vision more focused and a calmness began to settle on me.

"Sri, will you give my back a scratch?"

"Why? Is the Kayu Tas too precious for such use now?" she laughed.

"You have no idea what treasure you have in your hand"

"I have you, and isn't that enough?" I replied. "Go on, scratch my back!"

Chapter Twenty Three

I have no idea how long we spent with Badang as the days just flew by. He gave us little time for rest; it was either quietly being instructed in the arts of diagnosis and healing, or roaming the jungle, sometimes in the heat of the day and oftentimes in the depth of the night.

With this new power of sight from the dwellers of the Pokok Seruling, I was able to see the aura of whatever Badang pointed out to me. Plants that have power to heal showed a different aura to the plants that would do harm or those that were neutral in their existence. Some types of earth exuded a certain smell indicating a presence that could be extracted to help in healing.

As time passed and with Badang's teaching, Sri and I became as sensitive as he was. We could hear and understand the chatter of insects or the sighs of plants. Everything became alive, even the rocks could speak and the gurgle of each little stream told a story.

"Why did we not know of all these things before?" I wondered.

"You were all too proud to want to know. Mankind, through its ignorance, has walked by the treasures at his side or under his feet. We think we know it all and that is why we are deprived of this Paradise. Instead, we try to make one ourselves, like trying to invent water while ignoring the rivers and streams," explained Badang.

An overhanging bough of Kemuning swayed and laughed at his explanation and a rhinoceros beetle flew by muttering his disgust at the time wasted discussing Man.

Badang taught me that sometimes it was best to gather medicinal plants when their power is at its height. "Their aura gives a fair indication of their maximum potency. With their permission, one can gather their leaves or seeds or even the whole plant. It depends on the way you ask them and your given reason. Almost all plants give up their lives willingly for a good cause but it behoves the gatherer to ensure that the plant's progeny exists to continue its line."

I became learned in the fact that Nature was alive and eager to communicate with Mankind. She is always there and ready to help, if only Man would just listen and ask. Nature is still a patient Mother.

One day, we came across a sick gibbon on the trail. It must have fallen off a branch and broken its arm. It lay there, readying itself for its final end. Ants had already gathered by its fast-cooling body when we came across it.

"Si Jan, use your Kayu Tas," Badang ordered. I stood still, not knowing what to do. Badang took hold of the stick and placed one end of it on the broken limb. The gibbon stared at us as Badang started intoning certain sacred verses in the Khmer dialect, while waving the stick over the fracture.

The torn skin gradually closed after the protruding bones had shrunk back into the limb. The surprised animal clambered up the tree; looked back, it uttered a short line of thanks and went on its way.

"How did you do that?" we asked Badang. "The Kayu Tas is a useful tool in the transmission of energy, and the verses I intoned reversed Time so the two together effected what you may call … a cure. Though the gibbon, as far as he is concerned, never fell. You could see its surprised face wondering what the fuss was all about."

I had seen Aweh reverse Time for the blacksmith in Dacca before so I was not too surprised.

Badang held up a word of warning "Ah, but Time will ultimately catch up when its time for the gibbon to go. He will be found dead one day with a fractured arm, no doubt."

"Why did you not wave your hand over the gibbon's broken arm instead of using the stick?" I asked.

"Haven't you ever been bitten by a gibbon? Use the stick, stupid."

We realised that there was so much to learn from Badang. He read our thoughts and assured us that what we learnt would be more than enough to face the world when we went back to it. "Try not to show them too many things, for what they do not know, they will conspire to destroy. Humility is not in human nature. Be careful, Si Jan, do not lose yourself or Sri."

Another day we had a visitor. A man approached the border of our Fairy Realm. We saw him paddle his little sampan upstream, searching for Badang's hut. Being unsuccessful, he drew his little boat by the bank, knelt on the sand and cried out for Badang.

"Come, we'll go into Hari Kong and emerge behind him. Man must not know where we live, otherwise, we'll have to move inland again, into deeper jungle."

We did as told and the three of us stepped out of the Dark Curtain and stood silently behind the wailing man.

Badang touched him on the shoulder and the man recoiled in shock to see us there.

He turned and, still on his knees, begged for help.

"My wife is dying. Her skin has turned yellow and she is fast becoming skin and bone. Please help, she is the mother of our seven children, the youngest only two."

"How did you know my name?" Badang asked.

"Our son caught a Hill Mynah with bird lime sometime ago. It learnt to talk not long after we had her. Ever since my wife became ill, it said nothing but your name: 'Badang! see Badang!' and 'go up the river'. Out of desperation, I took the bird's advice and paddled upstream hoping to meet you somehow. If you are Badang, please help!" he implored.

Badang laughed. "What a bird! Getting me work when all I wanted was a day of rest. What's your wife's name?"

"Maimunah, Siti Maimunah" he replied.

"And her mother's name?"

"Zubaidah."

"Good, have you a bottle in your sampan?"

"Yes, I came prepared. And I brought you some salt and tobacco too," he replied eagerly, scrambling up to get to his boat.

"The empty bottle will do. Give Si Jan the salt and tobacco."

Badang filled the bottle with river water, and using the names of the two women given to him, started to chant. He sang of the beautiful mountains, the jungle, the flowers, the Earth and the clouds in the sky, and as he droned on, my mind read his thoughts and pictured the scene he had just painted .

What a beautiful canvas it became, as it took life and became vibrant and real.

Then he invoked the presence of the Heavenly Beings, the

Devas and the Devis, inviting them to be present in his mind's picture. With his two hands, he raised the bottle upwards and, with his mind, directed them all into the water.

The water in that old glass bottle became clear and the blue aura it emitted was there for all to see. "Now, give this to your wife, just a cup a day."

The man prostrated himself and cried, profuse with thanks and appreciation.

"We have done something good, so now we disappear," Badang mumbled as we stepped back into Hari Kong. The man, with his forehead on the ground giving thanks, never saw us leave.

Not long after that incident, Sri noticed a large bunch of freshly cut flowers, fruits and cakes, candles and kemiaan incense lit and laid out on the river bank below where the man had been.

"She must have been cured," Badang said when he saw the offerings.

"We'll just absorb the incense and leave the rest to the birds and animals."

"Hill mynahs?" Sri laughed.

"Gibbons! 'Wak... wak'!" I imitated their cry and the jungle responded in kind.

Chapter Twenty Four

One night, while listening to the rain in our own hut, Sri placed her hand over my mouth: "Shhh …….. just let the rain talk." For once, I kept quiet and waited for a message to come through. Sri, being more attuned to such dimensions, was before me in getting its message.

"The river, our river, will be in trouble in the morning. The Rain says that it will be poisoned by men in the morning to kill fish."

"Does Badang know?"

"Of course, the Rain would have spoken to him too."

I asked Sri what more she knew about Badang. "Well, he is our own Dukun or Medicine man, who is also an Orang Bunyiaan. He heals us and the world we live in."

"But, as I said before, you are all invulnerable, how can you be hurt?"

She laughed. “Invulnerable? Yes, but not like you. You became invulnerable with the Spirit of Cane in you through the help of the ‘were tigers’ of Korinchi. Our men are invulnerable through the knowledge of Badang. He knows of certain herbs that when drunk confer the same power that you have—only lasting, however, as long as the herbal potion is in the bloodstream.”

“What kind of herbs?” I asked

“Well there’s the *Pratil Kin Kook, Pratil Chek Sang* ….” she rattled off the names of these special herbs, all in Cambodian.

“ Okay, I believe you,” I stopped her and she laughed as she snuggled closer: “You must learn to speak Khmer too; just empty your mind and let me fill you with the knowledge of our people.”

Badang’s footsteps could be heard coming up the slope.

“Well, you two lovebirds, I guess you heard what the Rain said. There will be work for us at the break of dawn tomorrow, so go get some sleep.” We just heard his voice; perhaps he was too polite to come in the door.

I slept little that night and spent it listening to Sri’s quiet breathing. Moonlight streamed into our little hut and Sri looked more beautiful than ever with her head nestled in my arms. She smiled at a pleasant dream, and, like a little kitten, nudged her head closer.

Morning came with little warning when Sri shook me awake just as sleep was finally beginning to come over me.

"Si Jan, it's urgent, we must go," she said pulling me up.

Badang was already at the river bank with his parang, pointing up-river.

"There are men in boats ready to poison our river to catch fish. They are pounding the tuba roots now, our river will die if this is allowed to happen."

"Si Jan! Get some Mau San to help too!" he shouted as he untied his headband and allowed his hair to blow free in the wind.

For once, Badang looked the wild savage that Hollywood films like to depict, a cross between a Tarzan and Tonto, as he chanted his spells and whistled in intervals.

"Let it come!" he yelled "Let it come! Si Jan! What are you waiting for?"

I was at a loss to know what he wanted me to do. Sri came up to me and shouted above the din. "He wants you to help summon up a storm, Si Jan, a storm!"

Fat Aunt had introduced me many years before to the art of summoning storms, but with such Great Mystics and Fairies around me, there was little time for my Mau San magic and I had never put Fat Aunt's storm-summoning spells into practice. But the magic I had more recently gleaned from Munshi's books on the art of summoning a storm would certainly help.

A storm they want, well, a storm they'll get!

Standing on a rock by the riverbank with Sri watching me,

I drew the charms in the air with the two fingers of my right hand. I clapped three times after reciting the necessary spells and stamped on the ground with my left foot.

"*Ating Musukai*!" I shouted, the phrase I remembered from the book under the sea.

The sky took on a sudden change as dark clouds started to gather, then to turn clockwise using us as the eye of a gathering hurricane.

Badang whistled and waved at the wind with his parang as though urging it on with great urgency.

A roar approached us from below as a wave some ten feet high came up-river. Blown by our wind and strengthened by our magic, it seemed to have a mind of its own.

Badang appeared satisfied and patted me on my shoulder: "That wave will destroy all those boats, their baskets and nets, and the tuba."

"One should only take what one needs and not destroy the world for others. This world of yours will be destroyed in the same way by men like those upstream. You will have to create a bigger storm to destroy them in order to save the world when that time comes. Remember!" he added.

A sudden vision of my time under the sea with Munshi, the official serving Ratu Kidul flashed by. The three books, wrapped in tiger skins? He predicted that I would only get to choose one of the three."

Badang looked hard at me and asked me which one I would choose.

"The one to destroy the world? Or the one to start a new one?........or the one to return to the Light of the Stars?" Sri added.

I forgot that both of them could read minds.

"Well, if I choose the first one, wouldn't I be like the men upstream? And if I choose the second, wouldn't I have to destroy the world in the first place so as to rebuild it again?"

The two smiled as though waiting for my obvious choice.

Just then the storm abated and bright sunshine descended upon us. The river settled back to its original sluggishness and yellow butterflies were back on the sandbank.

There was no sign of any debris being washed down by the retreating waters. I could see no bits of broken wood or sail or net. The water was just as clear as it had been before our storm.

"Where are their broken boats? I see no sign of drifting debris or net?"

Badang smiled: "Did you see their boats before the storm? Did you see the men?"

"No."

"That event was happening a few hundred miles away while we chanted. We used this river of ours to cause a tsunami on that far-away river to save it from being destroyed by greedy men."

"You mean, what you do here can affect change hundreds of miles away?"

"Not only hundreds, but thousands of miles away. This place just represents whatever else in this world."

Sri calmed me down and sat me on the rock to explain further while Badang walked away searching for a piece of bamboo.

"Si Jan, Badang is not a Healer or Dukun in the ordinary sense of the word. He rarely goes out to heal anyone, even if they come to him. The man's sick wife that he helped the other day was just an exception—it was just a lesson for you."

"So, who does he heal?"

"The World, Si Jan. Badang lives here in this isolated part of our Fairy Realm so that he can heal the world. He does it the way you just saw. He rights the wrongs done by one nation of men on another. He balances the books, shall we say and makes sure that the World of Men is kept in some order. You must realise that whatever you do here, the world outside will be affected. This whole Realm represents what is outside."

Badang returned from his search for a stick of bamboo. "Found one strong enough to hang my clothes on."

"Badang, Sri just told me about your powers, is it true that you can heal from afar?"

He smiled and said he could.

"Will you show me?"

"Who is sick? Who do you know is sick, Si Jan?"

I thought of my own father.

"He is not sick, Si Jan. Its only the scars on his legs and those in his mind due to the Japanese torture that need healing. Watch!" and he stuck the bamboo cane into the river bank.

"Now this bamboo is your father, treat it well. Where would his legs be, Si Jan?"

I pointed to the lower length of the cane.

"Right, they were scarred by burning tar, weren't they? Yes, so let's rub those scars away, gently, gently." Badang stroked that portion of bamboo while muttering a small prayer.

"Now his mind..... although he is a forgiving man, he never got over the mental torture he suffered as a prisoner of war. Your prisoner of war!" Badang glared at me. Sri laughed at his sudden change.

I didn't know what to say but just kept my eyes on the bamboo. Badang looked at me, smiled and started to chant the same verses he had chanted that day he had helped the man with his sick wife.

This time he sang of the beauty of the mountains from countries far away, the Himalayas with their slopes covered in flowering rhododendrons of red, white and purple. He then went on to sing of the beauty of cascading waterfalls into pools of emerald-coloured waters, of parrots and peacocks all sporting a thousand hues. I looked on and I next saw him paint the picture of a small pagoda or pavilion overlooking that scene of Paradise.

Then, to my surprise, he brought out the image of my father in his mind and settled him in that little pavilion.

"He should feel the bliss that was denied him until now, and live out his days until you return home as the doctor he wanted you to be."

My heart was bursting with thanks and gratitude to this mystic. Badang of the Wilds, how could I ever repay him for helping me right the wrongs of two lifetimes? At last, I was able to undo the harm I had done to this man, my present father, prisoner of our Japanese Army, when I was Captain Ichiro Sato in my past life.

Badang sensed my predicament and laughed: "Take good care of that bamboo!"

Chapter Twenty Five

A couple of days after the incident on the river, Badang took out a drum from his hut, "Si Jan, it is time for you to meet the Sky Walkers."

The drum was a home-made affair, about two feet in diameter of stretched skin of an animal over a round wooden frame, made taut over a fire.

"Skin of a *kijang*, the barking deer, Si Jan," Badang said, walking past.

"Come, let's go further up the slope. There is a flat rock where we can do the drumming. Sri, have you the other things?"

Carrying a tray of flowers and incense, Sri nodded in reply.

We walked up the slope. It was a sunny day and it felt like we were on a picnic.

From our little plateau we could see the jungle below. It seemed to stretch on forever.

"This view can extend to the end of the Universe, it does not belong only to this part of the world. You see what you want to see, and you can see forever if you want to."

"What about the world being round and all that?" I asked.

"We are not of this world, stupid" Badang replied, while lighting up the incense.

Sri sat back and just smiled. She had a way of being an onlooker, saying little, yet knowing much.

Badang began to intone some sacred verses, many of them of which I had already committed to heart these last few days with his coaching. I learnt fast as each night when Sri and I were left to ourselves, she would repeat the chants to me to make sure that I remembered them well.

The fumes from the burning kemiaan incense rose as Badang chanted on. It reminded me of the time when we searched for the 'Spirit of Cane' with the two 'were tigers' of Korinchi.

Badang held up the drum and with a shout started slapping it in a slow rhythm, all the while looking up at the sky.

"Stand! Si Jan!" he ordered "and look!"

The sky darkened as the rain clouds approached us from afar.

"Is it going to rain?" I asked. Sri shook her head and pointed to something in the sky.

Far away, I could see a speck or two of something approaching. Badang's drumming became more hurried and intense as they came nearer.

"Sky walkers" Sri whispered while standing behind. "Si Jan, Sky Walkers, people of the sky."

Nothing prepared me for the sight that I was seeing. Two men, dressed in the garb of the *Bon Po Shamans* or the Necromancer of Nechung from Tibet danced on the clouds above us. They turned this way and that way in clockwise and anti-clockwise steps, all the time in tune with Badang's drumming.

Their robes appeared ancient, draped with rosaries of beads and shells and each wearing an apron of bone and topped by a large hat with feathers of pheasant and peacock.

They appeared immersed in their dance and oblivious of our presence.

"*On Chok Paleng ka Paleng!*" Badang cried out.

The two beings stopped their dance and looked down as though surprised to see us there.

"Speak to them!" Badang ordered and gave a heavy thud on my back.

Something became loosened in my being as words, words that I had never mouthed before, started flowing.

"*On Chok Paleng ka Paleng, itang ma Jan seng ating kong!*" I announced myself in their Sky language.

They looked at each other and laughed, expressing their approval.

"*Dang yang si bang Si Jan, dang yang si bang*—well done, Si Jan, well done."

I realised that Sri and Badang were as fluent in that language as I had become. Now that the hesitancy to speak in any tongue had been literally knocked out of me, words flowed in accordance with my thoughts, unhindered.

Perched over their cloud bank, they were happy to engage us in conversation as Badang drummed softly on.

They wanted to know more about me. Badang and Sri appraised them of my deeds and even mentioned that I had met Ratu Kidul, Queen of the Southern Seas.

They leaned out further to have a closer look, then, as though pre-arranged, stood up on the clouds clapped their hands and started their dance again but this time twirling further and further away from us before vanishing from sight.

Badang stopped drumming when the sky cleared and the sun shone.

"Now, Si Jan, you have friends above and below."

"And under!" added Sri.

From that day, I realised how simple it was to speak in any language. It has all to do with the power of the Mind. Break the bonds that tie and inhibit your efforts and you are in the Realm of whoever or whatever you want to converse with, without fear or embarrassment.

I had learnt so much from Badang about the world we think we live in, and the other worlds in our midst.

"You will need a drum," Badang announced when we returned to his hut.

"A drum can do a lot of the talking for you, as it can carry your thoughts with its sound, so it must be one that sounds like your Being. You can't have one that sounds like a woman or another man. So choosing the right one, or rather making the correct one is important, very important!" he warned.

It took a few days before Badang announced that the day had come to make me the drum.

"We will have to see where the skin for your drum might be"

"See?" I asked, still getting used to their ways. Sri smiled as she filled a pot with water and laid it on the mat. "Yes, Si Jan, we must first see otherwise, it will be a wasted trek." Badang answered while staring at the bowl of water.

"Ah, look, there's a skin waiting for you," he pointed to the surface of the water.

I stared hard at that reflection of the clouds in the sky, then realising my mistake, relaxed my gaze, and slowly, a scene evolved to show a jungle clearing with an old kijang or muntjac deer.

"He won't be long in this world, we'd better get to him before he breathes his last," Badang announced as he tied his parang to his waist and adjusted his headband.

Looking at the sky, Badang whistled to a bird asking for the direction of where the deer could be found. The bird responded: "Go left, over that ridge," it said, as it flew away.

"Are you sure?" I whistled at its disappearing form.

Badang clipped me on the head as Sri laughed at my mischief. "*Bodoh!*—stupid, only Man tells lies."

"*Dozo sumimasen,*" I bowed in apology trying to be Japanese again.

"*Donguri!*" he replied in Japanese, followed by, in perfect English: "What a bloody idiot!"

"Badang, were you at Oxford too?" I asked, trying to sound serious.

It took us less than an hour to find the clearing we had seen reflected on the water. The kijang was crouched on the ground as though waiting patiently for our arrival. He looked up at us as we approached but made no effort to run away.

Badang knelt down and stroked its back speaking to it as he did so.

"This young student of mine needs a drum. He is trained enough to use one so we ask you to allow us to proceed."

The deer looked at me and, resting its head on Badang's open palm, its eyes glazed over as it slowly slipped away.

Badang motioned me over and, pointing to the now lifeless

form at our feet, and asked me to proceed.

"Take the whole skin, but leave the body, the head and limbs. We will have to bury it at the base of that tree."

It is easy to skin a dead deer while it still warm. I removed the skin as fast as I could and, with it now rolled up, we proceeded to bury the carcass.

Now Si Jan, you will have to make your own drum. When it is ready, we will listen to see if it is you."

A familiar voice sounded behind us: "Wah! What are you trying to make him into, Badang? Another Siberian Shaman?"

"Aweh!"

The joy of seeing my old teacher and friend again was immense.

Chapter Twenty Six

"Will it take a few days for my drum to be ready? I asked when we reached Badang's hut.

"No time, Si Jan, you have to come away as soon as possible. That battle we arranged will be on soon," Aweh announced.

"Battle? What battle?" I asked them.

"The one we have been preparing you for. We chose you to represent us long before you were born, and now the time has come for you to face the other party, and, hopefully defeat the Evil Ones. They have someone to do the fighting for them," Aweh added making himself more comfortable on the grass mat.

"Come, we will have a meal before we move on. Sri, will you bring us something to eat?"

Sri, who had been silent all this while, left us for our little hut up the slope; one could see her displeasure at my imminent departure and the dangers that I would be facing.

"We chose you because you have lived so many lives walking the straight line and at times bearing the cost of upholding one's honour and deed." Badang who had been sitting quietly added: "We watched as you went through one lifetime after another, through trials and tribulations, each time coming through the ordeals that were thrown at you. Fate had planned that you will be strong enough for this day. Don't worry, we will be around to help you."

All their talk about my past lives meant nothing to me. I could only remember that last one, as Captain Ichiro Sato dying under that wooden watch tower somewhere in Burma.

I was more interested in my drum.

"Your drum?" Badang said after reading my thoughts. "Just go into the future and bring it here," he said nonchalantly.

Sri returned carrying a tray filled with a steaming pot of fish curry, rice and fresh fruit. I was too occupied with Badang's statement to ask how she managed to bring forth so much food in such a short time. But then, these are the Fairy Folks, the Orang Bunyiaans. I gave it no further thought but pursued Badang on his last comment.

"How can I have a drum in the future when I have not made it yet?"

"You skinned a deer, didn't you?"

"Yes, I did."

"You skinned it to make yourself a drum, didn't you?"

"Yes."

"So? When that thought and the start of that action was formulated, the drum would have been made and will be there for you in the future, when the time comes for you to have it."

"Now that you have no time, isn't it right that you can borrow a bit of the future and retrieve your drum, use it, then hold on to it until time catches up with you again?"

Aweh laughed out loud at my confusion, and Sri just smiled while laying out the food on the mat.

"You will learn more as you go along, Si Jan, first go into battle, defeat that adversary of ours and come back for more of Badang's teachings."

"Aweh, Badang, with all my respects to you two, if the future is already decided, then why should I need to go into battle?"

"*Oi! Okubyoo ka?*" Aweh asked in Japanese. "You a coward?"

"*Sodewa arimasen*—no I'm not, I am just curious."

Badang took over the explanation. "The Future, Si Jan, is formed as you move in Time. What the Future will be depends on how far you have moved in a particular direction to take on a form for you. Take your drum for example. If you have just chopped a few stalks of thick bamboo and then killed a deer, the future is likely to evolve into a scenario where you will be found cooking the deer meat using the bamboo stalks for the fire.

But, if you had set out with the idea of skinning a deer to make a drum, and making the bamboo into strips to stretch the skin for a drum, then the Future would have your drum waiting for you. Do you understand?"

"So, Si Jan, right now, you have not moved far enough for the Future to determine the outcome of your coming battle. You will have to prepare yourself in Mind, Body and Spirit before the Future will evolve, hopefully, in your favour."

Aweh lifted a finger to caution: "Don't forget, the Other Side has this knowledge too."

With that, Aweh reached out and drew out a Shaman's drum from thin air.

"Here, the drum that you finally made."

I held it in my hand. The drum was about two feet in diameter and resembled Badang's, but it had the feathers of our sacred Hornbill festooned on its rim. I gave it a tap and the drum answered.

"Sounds like you!" Sri exclaimed. "Yes, just like you, a show-off, hornbill feathers and all," Aweh added.

"Now you can use the drum to talk, rather to carry what's on your mind to reach anyone or anything anywhere. I think you have enough things with you to be a real Shaman, Si Jan." Badang patted me on the shoulder. "Let us have a good meal now before you leave us tomorrow."

"Tomorrow?"

"Yes," they all nodded.

I turned to see what had happened to the roll of skin I brought home. It was nowhere to be found.

Sri pointed to the drum: "It's there now, Si Jan."

That night, deep in my own thoughts, I prepared myself for this oncoming fight. Sri slept like a kitten after a saucer of warm milk. I prayed she did not read what was on my mind that night. And the rain fell.

Chapter Twenty Seven

I awoke to the overpowering fragrance of cempaka flowers. The scent was so heavy that I could hardly breathe.

"Sri ....Sri! Why the smell?" I asked. There was no reply from the still darkened room. The sun was just a line of light on the horizon of Forever.

I realised that instead of Sri, lying beside me in her place was a pile of cempaka blossoms fresh as though just gathered a minute ago.

I reached for Kyai Aweng, my keris, and realised that the one that Pak Samad had given me was beside it too.

What's happening? Where has she gone? I sat up, now more confused than terrified.

"Kriyat!" I yelled and the spear came into my hand almost immediately. Looking around I could see, with the brightening dawn that my drum was where I had left it against the wall and the Kayu Tas was beside it.

The sun reached into the hut with an urgency as never before. Its fingers of light, no more a brilliant yellow but an intense orange as though trying to say that something was pressing and that I should be out to see.

Dressed in our traditional costume of a warrior, I emerged from the hut to find the world that I once knew had changed dramatically. I found myself standing on a cloud bank. Bandang's hut was nowhere to be seen and the Forever Jungle was just an orange sea that stretched into Eternity.

A calmness came upon me, as it always did before the onset of a battle. I was calm when we were in Burma not so long ago when the British planes strafed and bombed us in our trenches, yet still we charged on. We were the Knights of Bushido, trained to keep our emotions in check.

In one sense, I had become a knight then. I was left there to fight a battle. I had no feelings of abandonment by my friends or by Sri. They had said that I was to be gone the next day; instead, they had left me–but that was simply another way of parting.

I felt ready as I stood there on the cloud bank. I raised up my drum and started my chant; as I did so, thoughts came flowing into me from nowhere, and the words that emerged were strangely not my own.

I sang of my past, a past I never knew as a Viking warrior,

then a Norse trader, a Spanish sea captain, a wool merchant from the Caucasus, a hermit from Tibet—the list went on. I was unable to stop as long as I drummed up my past lives. The drumming began to slow down when I was a Chinese scholar named Li Man Chung, and finally stopped when I mentioned that I was a Japanese Army Captain called Ichiro Sato.

It was not the words that were important, rather the thoughts that the drumming carried with it. A flashback of a Tarzan film I had seen not so long ago came to mind—how those natives talked through their jungle telegraphs, those "talking drums of Africa" now finally making sense.

I did not have long to wait as a reply came swiftly.

My unseen enemy spoke of being the Champion of his Elders, he was the Black Knight of some Kingdom I had never heard of, then of more victories in more battles as he fought through the pages of history.

As a young Shaman, with this flimsy drum, two kerises and a spear, I could only stand and listen as he drummed on about his past conquests.

But I smiled when I remembered what Pak Samad had told me so many a time: "What a man *was* is of no importance; what a man *is* now and what he *will be* in the future is all that counts."

I decided not to listen to his drumming and fixed my thoughts on the shoal of yellow butterflies on a sandbank by the river instead.

His drumming stopped and only the rush of the wind could be heard. I could see a few black specks approaching-the Sky Walkers! Some twenty of them making their usual dance motions, twirling this way and that, all in time with their own drumming. When they came nearer I could see that they were dressed in an identical fashion, and each carried a drum like mine.

"*On Chok Paleng Ka Paleng!*" I shouted in greeting.

"*Dang yang si bang Si Jan. Weng lok simai ting, wing chook ating mu*—Good, we are just here to watch your battle, Si Jan. We may help if you need us to."

I shook my head but thanked them. Maybe it was out of pride or ignorance, but I wanted a battle with this still unseen foe to be fought with my own strength and my own fighting skills. I had no fear.

The sky darkened. A flock of crows flew past cawing their hearts out as though the end were nigh. "Bring it or him on!" I shouted at the gathering storm cloud. "Bring him on!"

A voice beside me shouted, "Yes! Bring him on!" and laughed. Nothing prepared me for this shock, for standing beside me was myself!

Chapter Twenty Eight

We were dressed in the same way as a pair of Malay warriors, long-sleeved shirts and pants with folded sarongs wrapped around the middle, and each with a keris tucked in both front and back. He must have spotted me before I could him and so transformed himself to look like me, I reasoned.

"*Apa Khabar*?" he asked after my health. Before I could reply, his keris was out and came rushing at my chest.

I suppose it was some quick thinking on my part that saved me. *If he has powers like me, then he would know that weapons are useless on me, unless?....unless?*

I turned to my side and his keris just scrapped by, tore my shirt and drew blood! I was right. Our powers had deserted us and we were on our own.

I pulled out Aweh's keris and tried to do the same to him. He turned and countered with another stab in my direction; this time we both missed.

He jumped back, leaving some distance between us. With his right hand raised high, he shouted a command and a heavy halberd came from nowhere and the staff settled in his hand.

Kriyat did not disappoint me when I called. Armed with these long weapons, we fought like two madmen, stabbing and slashing at each other and then jumping away again before making another attempt at a kill.

It must have taken some time as I could hear the Sky Walkers almost hoarse with their cheering.

He must have realised that his halberd was a bit too heavy and I too agile for it to be of any use. He threw the weapon high up in the air and, as Kriyat did before, it just rose and, as though needing another breath, disappeared out of sight.

He then commanded his keris to change, this time into a Mandau, a headhunter's favourite and came charging.

I held on to Kriyat, the spear, with my left hand and changed Aweh's keris into my Kanemoto, that trusty Japanese blade known for its sharpness.

As he charged, screaming and becoming less and less like me as time went by, I began to realise that I might just defeat this so called Champion of the Evil Ones.

Kanemoto came down on his shoulder hard. I was hoping that it should have ended the fight there and then but he was still fast. Turning his body sideways, my blade managed to hack at his shoulder blade, just taking some skin and flesh.

A strange light shot from his eyes as he glared at me. He snarled as he swung the mandau at my neck.

I turned and moved even closer up to him rendering his sword useless at so close a quarter. I could smell his foul breath, this Thing who looked so much like me a moment ago.

"Keris!" I commanded Aweng to change itself into its original form. It did before I could finish the word, as though it knew what to do in such a situation.

I pushed the blade in deep and then made a side slash to enlarge the wound further and jumped away.

A volcano of gore must have exploded somewhere in him, he spouted venom and anger, his eyes bloodshot and his fangs exposed for the world to see.

Snarling, and making lunge after lunge at me, he only revealed himself to be what he was originally, this Champion of the Evil Ones. A monster kept for a thousand lifetimes by them and let out only when a battle needed to be fought. A source of so much evil, borne out of hatred and fury, fed by his Handlers with a diet of resentment, begrudgery and greed. It grew with each passing lifetime into such a Being that feared no man or beast, for it was both.

He charged at me again, this time his eyes glowing red and

screaming much like a mad man with its mouth frothing and still slashing with his mandau.

I kept calm, and if you were there, you would have thought, I was half asleep. I took my time, holding on to Kriyat, I sheathed Kyai Aweng, my keris and pulled out the Kayu Tas, that thin walking stick that I had tied to the shaft of my spear.

The monster may have had all my weapons, but he did not have what my Masters taught or gave me. Not all of it anyway. He did not have a Master like Badang and the Kayu Tas.

As he came near enough, the Kayu Tas flew out and slashed him on his back.

He bounded back, much like an injured animal. The keris wound on him had healed with whatever magic he was endowed with, but my little stick had done more harm than the blade.

It proved to be my fifty third card, the joker in my pack of surprises. He turned and bounded away from the scene. A cheer came from the Sky Walkers as they got up to follow the beast as it ran away.

"*Si Jan! Payang! Payang!*" They cried out to me. "Chase him! Chase him!"

I chased after it or him, and catching up, speared him in the back with Kriyat. He turned around and snarled as I closed in. Another slash on his back with the Kayu Tas changed him to his real self. No longer did he look like me, but something with scales and fins on his back and web between his fingers and feet. He looked surprised at the loss of his deception and the return of his true self.

We were now perched on the top of a mountainous cliff with a raging river below. The Creature gave me a look of intense hatred and, before leaping into the ravine, threw his Mandau at me.

Distracted by his looks, I was slow to avoid the blade. It cut me deep in the shoulder.

I felt the pain, much like the pain inflicted by those villagers with my own sword in Burma in my past life. Was this the beginning of another death?

You may call it a revenge of some sort, but I had promised myself that I did not want to die again. Do not ask me why or how. I had resolved that no one would ever kill me, I would only die if and when I wanted to, and now all I wanted was to kill this thing!

Sending Kriyat back, I leapt after him. The ravine must have been more than a hundred feet deep and as we went down, the spray and roar of the river came up to meet us as we crashed in.

It was a good swimmer. I could only allow the river to carry me along and just stayed afloat to keep an eye on this "thing" as it made its way towards the sea.

The river began to slow and the smell of the sea air came to meet me. The sun shone and a few seagulls, together with our

Sky Walkers, were the only spectators of this so called Battle.

Not long after, we came into real saltwater and away from the river mouth, the sea suddenly appeared calm and mirror like.

The Creature and I, just a few metres apart, paddled water and waited as we somehow knew what was to come next.

The sun lost its heat and the sea took on a strange shimmer. An area of water started churning and soon a funnel of water formed, allowing us to peer right down to the seabed.

The Creature was the first to dive in and I followed. Sliding on the walls of this green funnel, we reached the sea floor in no time. The Creature got up though limping badly made a beeline for the entrance of the palace of Ratu Kidul.

It snarled at the Royal Guards, pushing them aside and tearing at the seaweed curtains.

I followed its passage and before long we reached the Secret Library of 'Lost Books'.

Munshi, the Queen's scribe, barred the way shouting for it to leave. More heavily armed guards came, but were useless against this Creature. With a wave of his arm, many of the Queen's men were swept aside like a deck of cards.

Munshi made a rush at it, only to be struck down like the rest.

It then turned and ran towards the Queen's private chambers.

"Si Jan, he is after those three books!" Munshi managed to say when I finally reached him. He was in a bad state—I could feel the crackle of crushed bones as I cradled him in my arms.

"Forget about me, stop him from taking the books!" he screamed. "Stop him!"

I left Munshi with two of the men who arrived in time and ran towards the entrance of the chamber.

It had left a few mangled bodies in its wake. They were strewn on the ground like broken dolls. There was nothing much I could do for them and so I moved on.

I could hear the tearing down of doors and the crashing of ornaments or glassware as they fell on the floor. The creature growled and snarled as it rummaged around looking for the Books.

"They are here with me!" I lied. The creature stopped and approached me with a menace that only a demon could muster. Roaring hatred, it tore towards me with his arms outstretched and claws exposed ready to tear me to bits. Kyai Aweng, now drawn and ready for the final stab, buzzed with excitement.

I waited as the Creature came nearer. I could see that it had armed itself with a thirteen waved keris, the blade blackened with arsenic, ready to inflict a mortal wound on any adversary of his. Our powers of Invulnerability now neutralised and my powers to re-enter into Hari Kong probably dissolved, I knew it would be a fight to death with what was charging at me.

Steadying myself as the charge came, my flimsy stick, my saviour the Kayu Tas, flashed out from my left, slashing it across the chest.

It stopped for a moment and then charged at me again with his keris aimed at my heart.

Kyai Aweng, my blade forged from the red hot metal by Aweh's bare hands, flew to block its thrust.

Parrying his blade to the side, I managed to use Kyai Aweng to slash upwards and across the chest of this furious Thing.

I could see the gash of red opening as I stabbed Aweng deeper into its body.

It replied by thrusting his blade into my abdomen, leaving the keris in, it turned and ran deeper into the green wall of seaweed curtains.

I could hear it laugh its demonic laugh as it found what it was looking for.

The poisoned keris was gradually making itself felt as pain travelled in my innards and moving down towards my groin. I managed to pull out the evil blade. The stench of activated arsenic was overpowering.

Dragging myself towards where the laugh came from, I found an old Spanish sea captain's chest, probably one lost at sea from the time of the Spanish Armada. In it were the remaining two books, both with tiger skins as their covers.

"One has the ways to end this world, the other to mend it and the last to take us back to the stars"—words I remembered the Munshi saying not so long ago.

Which of the three books did the demon take?

"Take the one on your left, Si Jan," the voice of a lady whispered behind me. "Give it to someone on land, someone like Aweh. Keep the last book for yourself. That would be the book that had been meant for you," she added.

I looked back and came face-to-face with a smiling Queen Ratu Kidul. She was dressed in emerald green and bedecked with gold, emeralds and pearls. There was a greenish aura around her as she stood now flanked by all her retainers, most of them armed with halberds and trident spears.

Despite all the damage the Creature caused just a moment ago, those that I thought were killed by it stood next to the Queen and all were calm and even smiling. Munshi now restored to his former self approached me. "Si Jan, you have your Eighth Day or Hari Kong for healing and mending on land; we have our own here in the sea. Your wound appears serious, do lie on that couch and let us cure you."

With all the excitement around, I had forgotten about the wounds the Creature had inflicted on me—the deep cut on my shoulder and the now darkening wound in my abdomen made by his poisonous keris.

"The arsenic on the blade will kill if not removed in time," he said as he led me towards the couch.

The Queen Ratu Kidul whispered something to one of her men. He nodded in understanding and went back into the green curtain of seaweed.

With her whole retinue watching, the Queen approached me and, smilingly, examined the gash on my shoulder and nodded to the Munshi.

"We can mend that." And then looking at the fast discolouring wound in my abdomen, she shook her head: "This will need the help of Kring and Woyok—this is serious."

Am I now destined to die? And move on to another re-incarnation?

I had seen men die from wounds made by poisoned kerises, kerises like the one that the Creature used on me. Their deaths were slow and agonising. Maybe because of that memory, I felt the pain increasing and then a throbbing in my head. My eyes started to burn and the vision of the Queen and the Munshi became more hazy with each passing minute.

There was a commotion in the room when the retainer who had left the room some time earlier returned with a small casket in his hands. When opened by the Queen herself, two writhing things came out of the box.

"These are our two most poisonous creatures, the blue

ringed octopus and the sea snake. Their combined poisons will neutralise what is killing you now."

By then, I was almost unconscious and unable to understand how three poisons could restore me to some form of health.

The voices of those laughing Burmese villagers came back to haunt me. The perfume of Sri's cempaka flowers came back to torment me, to hurt me more. "Why did she leave?" Pictures of my loved ones in this lifetime—my parents, Fat Aunt, Chee, Pak Samad, Aweh and Badang—flashed through my mind.

I could feel the movements of that little octopus and the wriggle of the sea snake inside me before it all became dark and quiet. I awoke to see Munshi holding half a scallop shell filled with a blackish fluid. "This is what is left of the arsenic in you, the rest was absorbed by Kring and Woyok before they died." For a moment, I did not know what to say as I looked down at the two dead sea creatures on the floor.

"Si Jan, take the two books back to land. Give one to Aweh who will use it when the time comes. Keep the remaining one for yourself and those around you when your time comes too," added Ratu Kidul now seated behind my couch.

"Whatever happens on Land, Si Jan, the sea will always triumph. Mankind can do its worst but we will ultimately win. We have no need for these books, but have kept them safe until it is decision time for those on Land."

"You will live to see how Mankind behaves in the next thirty years or so, you will see what mess the Evil Ones will turn it into and you will see how the power of those opposing it will ultimately triumph. Do not go back to the Stars so soon, as the Mayans did before. You are destined for further clashes with the Evil Ones. Know that they will be waiting for you. Do not run, help Aweh. Stay to fight 'till you can fight no more."

Those were the last words I heard Ratu Kidul say as she somehow melted into the green curtains taking the whole retinue of followers with her.

Left with the Munshi, I felt totally alone once more.

"That is the way of the warrior, Si Jan. You must realise that to win, you must be detached. Detached from fear, detached from people, detached from love or hate and most importantly, detached from yourself," he said, as he helped me off the bed.

"Your reward, Si Jan, is in the last book. When you finally get to open it, the words now hidden will surface on the pages all by itself. There is no need of me or my finger. Use it and you will be able to return to the Stars with whomever you choose to bring with you."

Tears of another parting started to well up in me. I did not know what to say again as I looked at this ancient scholar from under the waves.

"Si Jan, know that we are the true guardians of this Earth, in the end, we will be the ones who will decide when it is time to wash it clean and allow Aweh to use his Book to rejuvenate the Earth again. By then, my young man, you should be ready to read your Book too."

"Munshi, with all respects to you. Why did you urge me to stop that Creature from getting at the Books a few moments ago, when you know it is unimportant because the Sea will always win?"

"I was afraid that he may have chosen the wrong one!" Munshi laughed, showing his aged teeth.

I laughed too. "Yes, I suppose you are right. What if he had stolen my Book? There would be wars and wars, and no way for me to go home."

Chapter Twenty Nine

There were no large turtles to give me a ride back to land when I came out of Ratu Kidul's Palace.

"Ride a waterspout, it will be faster," Munshi said giving my back a pat. "Just stand here and wait."

The green funnel of water still swirled around us and looking up, I could see the sky and the Sky Walkers peering down and laughing.

Now the direction of the swirling waters changed, going anti-clockwise the exposed sea floor gradually became covered and the rising waters lifted me up. The funnel slowly settled and became more level with the open sea, as I was lifted higher by the waterspout to a height almost level with the Sky Walkers' cloud bank.

"*Dang yang si bang! Si Jan! Dang yang si bang!*" they shouted in unison. "Well done!"

"*On chok paleng ka paleng, weng ko Aweh itui ka an tui yong esuk!*—My respects to you all, I am going to see Aweh and give him his Book!" I replied.

They bowed as though in consent, then turning around did their ritual of the twirling dance and were soon out of sight.

Perched atop the swirling waterspout, I managed to catch a Grey Wind as it blew towards me.

The sound of a drum could be heard in the distance. It was from the Creature that ran away from the fight. The drumming spoke of his victory in acquiring the Book and of his defeating me in battle. He went on to boast that they, the Evil Ones, would have the help of the world's leading politicians and greedy businessmen and would one day dominate the Earth and destroy anyone who serves the Light.

But as I knew what the final outcome would be, I just smiled as the Wind carried me towards the Malayan heartland.

I neared the flat rock not far from Badang's hut, and saw a small crowd waving as I drew closer.

"*Anyang Baling Katimu!*" and the Wind slowed to allow me to fall into the open arms of Aweh.

"You did it!" he shouted. There was much laughter all around as the Grey Wind moved away and the excitement of the occasion settled somewhat. I began to realise who the people around me were.

"Fat Aunt! You finally came!" I yelled, for once forgetting myself. "How could I miss this joyous occasion?" she replied, hugging me hard with her flabby arms. "I am proud of you. We are all proud of you!" she added.

Rashid, my father's old chauffeur, was behind her, smiling and saying nothing.

"Rashid! Are you one of us too?"

"What do you think?"Aweh said. "He looked after you in secret while you were growing up, just to make sure that none of the Evil Ones would get to you before you were ready to become one of us."

I suddenly remembered the day that Rashid mentioned the 'Spirit of Cane' when I was just a boy. How could he have known about it if he were not a mystic? I realised then how much I owed him. He had been there to protect me and see that I grew up safe. I gave him a hug and thanked him. I could see a tear welling in his eye. He smiled and said nothing.

Pak Samad came up next, patting me on my back. "Jepun, you did well. You have the Book for Aweh? Yes, that is good, and I believe you have one for yourself?"

I showed him the two books and he nodded. "Give that one to Aweh and keep that for yourself, as you have been told. Use it only at the right time. No running away as the Mayans, the Tangyuks or the Patinggis did."

"Who were these Patinggis, Tangyuks and all?"

"They are People from the Past, who went *en masse* into the Light when the going got tough. You, Si Jan will have to stay and fight to restore the Balance. Stay beside Aweh and his friends. We will all be behind you."

"Where is Sri?" I asked anxiously. Badang patted me on the shoulder. "Jepun, Sri returned to the Princess so as not to distract you when you went into battle—battles must be fought on your own with an undisturbed mind. To be successful as a warrior, there should be no space for love, worry, longing or hatred. She left while you were asleep, leaving behind a pile of cempaka flowers; each blossom had been handpicked by her before she went away."

I was glad to understand why she had left me, for I would not have succeeded in fighting the Creature with half my mind on her and whatever else.

"Don't worry Jepun. She will be there waiting for you with the Princess and the others," Pak Samad assured me.

"We will celebrate, eat and dance like we have never danced before!" Aweh announced.

"Before we leave, Pak Samad, shall I reply to that Creature's drumming?"

"Why not?"Aweh said, before Pak Samad could reply. "Go on, give them a taste of what is to come!"

I had been dying to reply to that Thing ever since I stepped on to dry land. From the thin air, I drew down my drum.

"We know that you have that First Book. We know that you will not live long, as your injuries can only be cured by us. We have the Second Book, the knowledge within will neutralise all the Evil you can do. The Sea will ultimately triumph. And, the Sea, is on our side. I repeat, the Sea, is on our Side!"

Fat Aunt clapped, while the rest slapped me on the back.

"Well drummed, Jepun. Well drummed!" Pak Samad said. "Shall we go now?"

"Let's ride the Grey Wind?" I suggested.

"Ride the Grey Wind, he says! We all know that you are dying to see your Sri, but how could your Fat Aunt ride the Grey Wind?" Aweh asked. "There would be one almighty splash if she falls off!"

With that, Pak Samad made a slit into the Hari Kong and we all entered it, still laughing.

The End

Background Information

Keris: The keris is quintessentially a weapon peculiar to the peoples of Indonesia, Malaysia, Brunei and the Southern Thailand.

Often viewed as a talisman more than a weapon, many kerises are believed to contain a Spirit or Guardian that will protect its owner. It may warn of imminent danger by rattling in its sheath or by other omens, like dreams, but it may also cause the owner harm if not treated with due respect.

Until the beginning of the last century, no man was considered dressed if seen without a keris on his person. These days, they are still worn on ceremonial occasions.

A keris blade may be sinuous, with waves like a moving snake or straight. The patterns on the blade suggest the type of power that the keris may possess.

A man's keris may be used to represent him if he is unable to attend in person.

Kukri: A weapon of the Nepalese and carried by their famous soldiers, the Gurkhas.

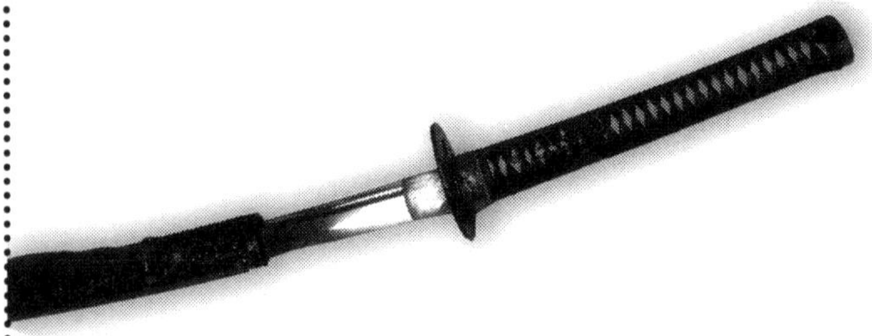

Kanemoto: Name of a famous swordsmith in old Japan. His blades are known for their extreme sharpness and strength.

Mandau: A head hunter's sword from Borneo, usually with bunches of a victim's hair on the scabbard.

Printed in Great Britain
by Amazon

35722717R00104